A THOUGHTFUL SOUL

A Thoughtful Soul

REFLECTIONS FROM
SWEDENBORG

Edited and Translated by George F. Dole

Foreword by Huston Smith

CHRYSALIS BOOKS

IMPRINT OF THE SWEDENBORG FOUNDATION

WEST CHESTER · PENNSYLVANIA

Chrysalis Books is an imprint of the Swedenborg Foundation, Inc.
For more information, contact:

Chrysalis Books
Swedenborg Foundation
320 N. Church Street
West Chester, PA 19380

Library of Congress Cataloging-in-Publication Data

Swedenborg,Emanuel, 1688–1772.
A thoughtful soul: reflections from Swedenborg / edited by George F. Dole.
p.   cm.
Includes bibliographical references.
ISBN 0-87785-148-4
1. Theology. 2. Philosophy. I. Dole, George F. II. Swedenborg, Emanuel,
1688–1772. View from within. III. Title.
BX8711.A7D65 1995
230' .94–dc20   95–6651

Edited by Mary Lou Bertucci
Designed by Laury A. Egan
Cover photograph by Laury A. Egan
Typeset in Galliard and Helvetica

Printed in the United States of America

Affectionately dedicated to Jim Fadiman,
whose thoughtful suggestion led—eventually—to this book

By birth, we are all gifted with the ability to discern what is true even to that deepest level where angels of the third [highest] heaven are. . . . So we can become rational as our discernment is raised. . . . If the love of our intentionality is not raised at the same time, then no matter how high our discernment's wisdom may rise, it eventually falls back to [the level of] its love.

Divine Love and Wisdom 258

CONTENTS

.

CONTENTS

FOREWORD

by Huston Smith

·

Postmodern philosophers, though often critical of modern (seventeenth to nineteenth century) epistemologists, continue to accept Immanuel Kant's dictum that we *know* only where our concepts are validated by sense reports. I think of a tree. Is that thought true, or is it simply a figment of my imagination, like a unicorn? The answer depends on whether my physical senses—in this case, sight and touch—assure me that trees exist.

This bears on this new book on Emanuel Swedenborg by indicating his importance. A number of Kant's followers were also admirers of Swedenborg, some to the point that they pressed Swedenborg's writings on him. Kant's reactions are instructive, for they show this most level-headed and composed of philosophers in one of the rare moments when, in current idiom, he "blew his cool." Swedenborg's firsthand reports of higher worlds clearly upset Kant. "What astonishing consequences would follow," he wrote, "should the philosopher make room in his philosophy for even one [of Swedenborg's visions]!" Astonishing, indeed, for the consequence would be nothing short of the collapse of Kant's entire earthbound, sense-grounded epistemology, which continues to rule the philosophical roost.

This book doesn't prove that Swedenborg's alternative view of knowledge—more generous in not tying it exclusively to sense experiences—must be accepted, but it does underscore two facts. First, ways of knowing are decisive in determining the worlds they open onto: a blind man's world is a world without light. Second, Kant's restriction of knowledge to the domain of sense experience is arbitrary. If there are exceptional individuals who can perceive metaphysical objects as directly as normal people perceive physical objects, an epistemology more generous than Kant's is required to take account of them.

The contemporary world isn't very open to the prospect of there being seers in the literal sense of that word: people who possess the "Third Eye" that Buddhists speak of and who actually see metaphysical entities. But savants do exist. That Thomas Fullers, a Virginia slave who could barely do more than count, could in a minute and a half calculate how many seconds a man who was seventy years, seventeen days, and twelve hours old had lived, not forgetting to enter leap years into his reckonings (2,210,500,800 is the answer) defies explanation. In music, we have Mozart, regarding whose talent critics can finally say only that it came "from beyond." And there have been wizards in other fields as well. Given the inexplicability of such talents, it seems arbitrary to rule out the possibility of metaphysical savants, among whom—along with Jacob Boehme, William Blake, and Rudolf Steiner—Emanuel Swedenborg must be numbered among the greatest.

To credit Swedenborg as such a prodigy, we needn't believe every detail of his reports, for vision can be reliable without being 20:20. Still, the consistency in what he tells us and the way his visions seem to have empowered rather than interfered with his life suggest that the outlines, at least, of his descriptions are accurate. That conclusion gains force when we note the extent to which Swedenborg's reports—again, in their broad outlines—conform to those of history's other great visionaries.

To readers who may be meeting Swedenborg for the first time in these pages and find his almost garrulous talk about angels initially offsetting, let me confess that I too went through that phase. Fortunately, however, I checked my annoyance by asking why clear-minded, well-balanced people like D.T. Suzuki and literary giants of the stature of Jorge Luis Borges and Czeslaw Milosz refused to let the imperious demands of common sense derail them and kept on reading this author. It did not take me long to conclude that it was their alertness to the largeness of life itself—its largeness and mystery—that rescued them from the rules of intellectual respectability and allowed Swedenborg's more generous world of discourse to have its rights.

"If only people knew that we are all born for heaven," we read in these pages, together with the assurance that "we are accepted into heaven when we accept heaven into ourselves." How good those assurances sound in our dark and troubled time. George F. Dole, the editor of this work and translator of the passages from Swedenborg's original Latin, has done us a great service in bringing Emanuel Swedenborg back to the attention of our distracted age.

PREFACE

·

At a meeting of persons involved in transpersonal psychology some years ago, Jim Fadiman responded to the news that I was a "Swedenborgian" with a plea that the formidable mass of Swedenborg's writing be made more accessible. The consequent effort to sort Swedenborg's thought into contemporary categories reinforced my conviction that the whole purpose of his theological output was to help humans move toward being more truly and profoundly human—to convince us that we are indeed souls, now and forever, and to inspire us to be thoughtful ones.

Swedenborg did this with care, at length, and in the language of his times. My selection of ideas from Swedenborg's theological works is based on the assumption that there are, so to speak, two distinguishable avenues of approach to his theology. There is the particular Christian theme, stressed (understandably) in the church institutions that arose after his death. However, there also is a strong metaphysical or universalizing theme that gives a unique cast to his Christianity. Swedenborg insists, for example, that "the good [people] of all religions are saved" and is much kinder to "gentiles" than to traditional Christians. This aspect of his thought has been appreciated by such creative nonconformists as Johann Wolfgang von Goethe, William Blake, and Samuel Taylor Coleridge.

There is no question that, for Swedenborg, the Christian model was the most complete and appropriate. There is also no question that he saw Christianity as radically misunderstood in his own times, as having been bent to human institutional needs. Divorced from its universalizing ground, Christianity readily lapsed into sectarianism and nutured the worst rather than the best in human nature.

For this edition, I have presented, overall and in each chapter, the broadest context first and have moved into the realm of specifically Christian concepts only after that context is in place. I hasten to add that I have moved only a very little way into the wealth of detail of Swedenborgian theology. There is scarcely a statement of principle in the following pages that could not be annotated at considerable length. In my introduction, I offer a biographical sketch to help the reader understand how Swedenborg came to his theology and to introduce the man—the eighteenth-century Swedish scientist, politician, and mystic—who devoted the last thirty years of his life to timeless issues.

Throughout this edition, I have translated Swedenborg's term *charitas* as "compassion" rather than "charity." While I must apologize for the rather wooden consistency with which this is done, I find the former word used more and more to indicate the kind of heartfelt and active response to human need that the Latin *charitas* clearly intends and am also aware that "charity" is commonly used in a more limited sense, sometimes with implications of condescension.

I am grateful to a number of people who have helped me in my revisions. The Rev. Donald L. Rose responded to my requests with some very valuable suggestions. Louise Woofenden made a number of most accurate and helpful comments on my translation of Swedenborg's original Latin, which have, I trust, been heeded. At the suggestion of Carol Lawson, I have added introductions to each chapter to place the extracts of Swedenborg's writings in a context and so to lighten the reader's task. These prefaces have benefited from a number of suggestions made by John L. Hitchcock. I also wish to thank the Swedenborg Foundation for its support throughout the writing process; its publications committee for constructive suggestions along the way; Harvey Bellin for urging the inclusion of the biographical sketch in my introduction; and especially Mary Lou Bertucci, editorial surgeon and disarming correspondent. In addition, I am grateful to

Elizabeth Pitt, the Swedenborg Foundation librarian, for the precise and exhaustive indices.

Finally, I am particularly grateful to Alice Skinner for her insistent initiative toward the revision of this work. I have a sense that she is looking over my shoulder as I write. Hers is a welcome presence.

George F. Dole

Sharon, Massachusetts

INTRODUCTION

.

If we take "the present" as a fixed point of reference, to which "the past" and "the future" are relative, we can distinguish three complementary modes of knowing. We see the present with a particular kind of directness and certainty but often with a sense of ambiguity as to meaning. We see the past more remotely and selectively but with a much clearer sense of its patterns. We see the future more remotely still, with a view shaped by our sense of patterns and colored by our hopes and fears—very hazy as to detail. Part of understanding ourselves as individuals and part of understanding each other involve grasping how these three modes interact in the consciousness of the "self."

To understand Emanuel Swedenborg's life as he lived it, we must try to move out of our retrospective view, to be aware of what was present, past, and future to him as his story progresses. In his later years, Swedenborg believed that everything before 1744–1745 was preparation for his mission as a revelator, but this view cannot be retrojected into the "preparation" itself. Perhaps insidiously, those who find his thought relevant to the twentieth century may forget that Swedenborg was addressing his own eighteenth-century readers and may neglect their own responsibility to distinguish the timeless from the timebound.

To provide a focus for this overview, I would highlight, first of all, Swedenborg's extraordinary intellect and, second, his intense devotion to two causes—the religion of his upbringing and the science of his university education. At the beginning of the eighteenth century, Lutheran orthodoxy and Cartesian science were parting company. This was a painful process, with clerics seeing the authority of the church undermined and scientists seeing the church as the primary obstacle to freedom of inquiry. It was a process that Swedenborg internalized.

In his own home, religion was the dominant theme. His father, Jesper Swedberg, was a Lutheran clergyman with a good deal of evangelical fire (Queen Ulrica Eleonora ennobled the Swedeberg family in 1719, changing the family name to "Swedenborg"). Eventually, Jesper would become a bishop, in and out of hot water with the church for his efforts to revise the hymnal along more pietistic and less orthodox lines. Theology was apparently standard conversational fare at the dinner table. It is also significant, however, that the family had substantial interests in the mining industry, mining being the mainstay of the Swedish economy. We may suspect that the family properties were a persistent minor theme.

Jesper was on the faculty at Uppsala University when his son matriculated there at the age of eleven (not all that unusual an event); but, shortly thereafter, he was made bishop of Skara and moved to his new charge. At this time, Emanuel moved in with his older sister and her new husband, Erik Benzelius, who felt himself to be at the forefront of the Cartesian revolution and who, as university librarian, was very much aware of the latest scientific publishing.

In one sense, it was a period of truce for science and religion. Charles XI had decreed just a decade earlier that science was not to make pronouncements on matters of doctrine and that the church was not to restrict scientific inquiry. It was perhaps only this rudimentary compartmentalization that enabled Swedenborg to pursue a scientific rather than a theological course of study without causing a serious rift with his father.

Swedenborg was graduated from Uppsala University in 1709, and the following year he set out on an extended trip abroad. At this time, England, France, and Germany were centers of scientific progress, but Sweden was relatively behind the times. In London, Swedenborg studied the work of Sir Issac Newton, worked with the astronomer John Flamsteed, and investigated Matthew Boyle's chemical experiments. Next, he traveled to the continent, making diplomatic contacts and focusing to some extent on mathematics. When he returned home, it was with a portfolio of mechanical inventions including a submarine, an airplane, and a stove, and with dreams of founding an observatory that would give Sweden a prominent place in the field of astronomy. In addition, on his trips abroad, he made a practice of lodging with artisans and picking up their skills, which came to include lens grinding, bookbinding, and cartography. Indeed, throughout his long life, even though he eventually settled into a comfortable house in Stockholm and enjoyed his garden, he spent a good deal of time abroad. In regard to his later publications, it was far easier for him to publish in Amsterdam and London, where the presses were not subject to ecclesiastical censorship, than in Stockholm. He wrote in Latin in order to reach out beyond the confines of Sweden, so language was no problem. He also published his larger scientific works in Dresden and Leipzig, both because of the superior quality of the presses there and because this gave his works access to the larger learned world of the continent.

Unfortunately, Swedenborg returned at a low point in Sweden's history. The charismatic Charles XII had made a spectacular attempt to extend the Swedish empire by conquest and had met disaster at the hands of Peter the Great. The cost of Charles' campaigns had been ruinous, and Sweden's economy was in a shambles. There was no realistic chance of Swedenborg's realizing his dream of an observatory. Ultimately, he found work as assistant to Sweden's foremost inventor, Christopher Polhelm, and became what we would now call a civil engineer.

With the support of the king, he then was appointed to a non-salaried position on the College of Mines—roughly the equivalent of the Department of the Interior. He toured the mining and smelting industries of Europe and published what turned out to be a definitive work on metallurgy. There were separate volumes on iron and copper, with an introductory volume laying philosophical foundations for physics and chemistry. This first volume, known most briefly as *The Principia*, included both a carefully worked out nebular hypothesis and a theory of matter as composed of patterned energy.

His life seemed pretty much on course at this point. He was profoundly disappointed to be still a bachelor after two courtships that had not worked out, but he was an accepted member of the government at the cabinet level with an international reputation in the field of metallurgy.

The next major turn of events in Swedenborg's life came shortly after his father's death when he began to use his spare time "in search of the soul." This was not an uncommon pursuit, but his approach was distinctive. Rather than theorize, he chose to undertake a very thorough study of human anatomy. If the body was indeed the kingdom of the soul, he reasoned, then that is surely where we should look. He spent time in dissection rooms in Paris but eventually decided to rely more on the published results of other researchers so that he might not be biased by his own first-hand discoveries.

The result of this study was two substantial volumes that included such substantial discoveries as the functions of the ductless glands and the localization of certain motor functions in the cortex of the brain. At the end, though, he had to rely more on doctrine than on the scalpel for his conclusions about the soul, and he regarded the whole massive work as having failed in its primary purpose. Characteristically, he decided that he simply had not been thorough enough and set out to do it right the second time. He now projected eleven volumes, of which he actually published two, with substantial parts of others left in draft.

He apparently began on this massive project in 1741, at the age of fifty-three. As he worked, he started to have experiences of "photism," mentally visible flashes of light or flame that, he came to realize, signalled his having arrived at some particularly significant insight. He began his "prologue" to the first volume of the new series by describing a kind of inborn rational instinct for the truth, an assertion potentially at odds with the strict empiricism he had previously insisted on.

Swedenborg was on the verge of an immense and traumatic

change. As he proceeded with the project, the conviction grew that it simply was not going to succeed. He began at about this time to record his dreams and to speculate on the guidance they offered. In his record of these dreams, we see a man struggling with his intellectual pride, with his alienation from his feelings, and with his distance from his childhood faith. On Easter weekend of 1744, this crisis issued in a mystical Christ vision of uncommon power. After a year of further struggle, a second vision, again at Easter time, left him with the conviction that he had been called to a new career.

The event is worth sketching. The vision took place in a London inn where he was having dinner and began with the appearance of a shadowy figure in the corner who told him emphatically not to eat so much. Later that night, he was awakened by the same figure, who identified himself as the Lord Jesus Christ and informed him that he was being commissioned to disclose the inner, spiritual meaning of the Bible. After this, Swedenborg reported, heaven and hell were opened to him. From that time until the closing days of his life, Swedenborg had almost daily "waking visions" of the spiritual world, including extended conversations with angels and spirits.

Swedenborg took his commission seriously, reviewing his university Hebrew and Greek and drafting his own extensive index of Bible passages. He began writing a Bible commentary, posthumously published in nine volumes as *The Word Explained*, but left it incomplete. From 1749 to 1756, he published a multi-volume work known as *Arcana Coelestia*, whose full title might be translated "A Disclosure of the Heavenly Depths in Sacred Scripture or the Word of the Lord." This work proceeds verse by verse and often word by word through the books of Genesis and Exodus, interpreting the narrative as a kind of parable with levels of meaning dealing with the spiritual history of humanity, the issues and course of the individual's spiritual pilgrimage, and deepest of all, the story of the interaction between the divine and the human sides of Jesus.

While he had begun with the explicit intent of covering the

whole Bible, he changed course after finishing his exegesis of Exodus and published, in 1758, five works of a very different nature. One was a very slender work, little more than a pamphlet, on the inhabitants of the planets. Another, *The New Jerusalem and Its Heavenly Doctrine*, was a survey of the main points of his theology organized in brief discussions of its commonest terms. A third—perhaps the most startling—was a small work called *The Last Judgment*, in which he described having witnessed this event in the spiritual world. A fourth, again more booklet than book, made his case for the existence of deeper meaning in scripture; and the fifth, *Heaven and Hell*, presented the nature of the spiritual world as he had experienced it. It seems clear that he was trying to put his theology in the most accessible form possible; and, in fact, *Heaven and Hell* has been the most popular of his works.

On completion of these 1758 works, he returned to the task of Scripture commentary and drafted most of a commentary on the last book of the Bible, Revelation. Knowing now that he would not be writing separate works on much of the rest of Scripture, he did a great deal of gathering of related passages and sketching their interpretation. The resulting work, *The Apocalypse Explained*, was never finished and was published only after his death.

In 1763 and 1764, he published another cluster of separate works. Four of these were on specific theological topics: *The Doctrine of the Lord*, *The Doctrine of Sacred Scripture*, *The Doctrine of Life*, and *The Doctrine of Faith*. One was a kind of sequel to his little work *The Last Judgment*, and two were companion volumes entitled *Divine Love and Wisdom* and *Divine Providence*, respectively. *Divine Love and Wisdom* presented his metaphysics in its broadest and least sectarian form, while *Divine Providence* brought this "down to earth," in a sense, in an effort to reconcile his experience of the beauty of the divine nature with his experience of a world full of violence and injustice. He then returned to the book of Revelation and published a relatively concise commentary, *The Apocalypse Revealed*.

His next project was a departure from previous policies in

another direction and resulted in his most controversial work, whose title has been variously translated as *Marital Love, Conjugial Love, Marriage Love, Love in Marriage,* and, most recently, *Married Love.* It is intriguing to see him talking about the inner differences between the sexes on the basis of his encounters with them in the spiritual world and also to see a combination of a highly idealistic view of marital fidelity and devotion on the one hand and a remarkably nonjudgmental attitude toward deviations from this ideal on the other.

The work on marriage was published in 1768, by which time Swedenborg was eighty years old. He was to publish just three more works. One was a booklet under the title *The Intercourse between the Soul and the Body;* one, a small and quite polemical critique of traditional Christian theology called *A Brief Exposition of the Teaching of the New Church;* and the third, the work that has been seen as his final summary, *True Christian Religion.*

It has been my own contention, though, that this final work is less a summary than an effort to demonstrate that this theology is truly Christian. Two of his earliest followers, both clergymen, had been accused of heresy, and the ecclesiastical inquiry had shifted focus from what these men themselves had written to the works of Swedenborg himself. Perhaps there was a bit of his father's evangelical fire left in the old man, for he entered into the fray with a will.

Swedenborg died in 1772 in London. His had been a life remarkable for its energy and productivity but even more remarkable for its evolution. In retrospect, he seems never to have rested content with his achievements or his understanding but always to have pressed deeper. Through years of experience that have caused later generations to question his sanity, he remained both gracious and grounded. He was socially accessible and "low key" and remained a very effective member of the Swedish Parliament to the end of his life.

With this thought in mind, I designed this book to be an accessible introduction to Emanuel Swedenborg's thought, using his own words. In the Swedenborg Foundation's Standard Edition of Swedenborg's writings, those words, as translated from Latin, fill thirty volumes, so a single, slight book must necessarily be selective. The present selection of passages is deliberately chosen and arranged to address the spiritual questions of this late twentieth century, when mechanistic and exclusively materialistic accounts of reality are being challenged. Principles of complementarity, indeterminacy, chaos theory, and holography mix with rediscovered age old traditions of meditation and healing to offer a sometimes bewildering array of alternative views of our cosmos. I offer Swedenborg as a neglected resource in these times, of particular value because he stood on both sides of the great divide as a hardheaded scientist who had extensive spiritual experience.

Digests and summaries of Swedenborgian theology are too numerous to mention. The clearest "ancestor" of the present work is probably *The Gist of Swedenborg* (1920), compiled by Julian Smyth and William Wunsch This work was addressed to readers who were biblically literate and thoroughly familiar, though not necesssarily satisfied, with mainstream Christianity. Three quarters of a century later, there is a large audience that does not fit this description.

As to the arrangement of the present material, I felt it essential to begin by recognizing Swedenborg's awareness of limitations on our abilities to "know." If we take Swedenborg's words as the revelation they claim to be, it is all too easy to forget those limitations and drift into dogmatism. However, he is abundantly clear and insistent that there is no such thing as absolute objectivity, especially in spiritual matters. This does not mean there is no such thing as certainty— just that there is no necessary connection between certainty and truth. We can be dead certain and dead wrong at the same time. Our affections, moods, and purposes color not only our interpretations of our perceptions but even the perceptions themselves. In particular, the section on "Doubt, Reason, and Faith" in the first chapter is offered as Swedenborg's own "indeterminacy principle."

The second chapter, "Holistic Reality," goes directly to the largest context of our perception and understanding, looking at the oneness and interconnectedness of the cosmos. In a sense, this awareness follows David Bohm's insight that, if we would engage in the radical rethinking that physics seems to be demanding, we should start not with the observable "parts" of our experience but with the oneness we intuit as underlying them all (*Wholeness and the Implicate Order*, 1980). Chapter 3, "Alternate Realities," explores the substantiality and nature of spiritual reality. To my mind, these two concepts, that of "distinguishable oneness" and that of the reality of spirit, pervade the whole Swedenborgian system and give a distinctive cast to even the most familiar of subjects. At this very general level, too, we may see the clearest affinity with concepts of contemporary physics on the one hand and with interests of contemporary spirituality on the other.

The existence of alternate realities has implications for our own immortality, and this leads to consideration of ourselves as individuals how we are put together, so to speak, in chapter 4; how we may grow and change over the course of our lives, in chapter 5; and what constitutes a truly good life, in chapter 6. At this point, then, we have come from the cosmic overview down to the particular decisions of daily living, and the presentation turns around and heads back toward the universal. Chapter 7, "Correspondence," begins by looking at a central principle of Swedenborgian thought, the principle that every material entity or process is the result and, therefore, a mirror of some spiritual entity or process. This is both the "language of creation" and the language of revelation. In other words, Swedenborg insists that material things and processes are modeled on spiritual ones, making the visible world a means of access to understanding the invisible one. The next step is, then, to look at revelation as it happens on the individual and on the epochal scale. This is the subject of chapter 8.

Swedenborg would see it as no coincidence that communities tend to form around bodies of revelation, for the essential purpose of revelation, in his view, is the formation and nurturing of genuine community—spiritually seen, "a heaven from the human race." Chapter 9, therefore, samples what he has to say about spiritual community, including some comments on organized religion. Remarkably for his own time and seminally for ours, he sees divine purpose in religious pluralism.

The final chapter deals with the Divine, with the concept of God. It is hoped that, by coming at this vital topic in the context of what has preceded, the reader may do so with as little as possible of the baggage that has become attached to God language over the centuries. While the more traditional sequence of presentation (as in *The Gist of Swedenborg*, for example), is to begin with this material because of its centrality, it seems at least as reasonable to regard it as a goal to be sought rather than as a place to start.

The introductory remarks to each chapter explain why its particular material has been selected and how these ideas relate to what has preceded. If this does nothing else, it should help alert the reader to my bias—a bias that, frankly, I hope the reader comes to share.

A THOUGHTFUL SOUL

CHAPTER 1

How We Know

.

Sometimes I wonder how strict determinism accounts for the extraordinary range of human opinions. Brilliant minds have been certain of the existence of God, and other equally brilliant minds have been just as certain that such belief is folly. If all our thoughts are determined by what has happened to us, where does error creep in? There must be a fuzziness somewhere. Somehow, it must be possible for us not to be affected by things that have happened, or to be affected by things that have not happened. We must be able to perceive things not exactly as they actually are. "Fuzzy logic" is for real.

In Emanuel Swedenborg's thought, this is an essential characteristic of the physical world. He prized human freedom and insisted that, if that freedom is to have any meaning at all, it must include the freedom to call evil good and good evil. The free mind must be free to err; or, in more personal terms, the only truth that is fully accepted is the truth that is freely chosen.

As a scientist, Swedenborg had posited an ideal "pure intellect," an intellect elevated above the emotions so as to see reality with total clarity. Once he began to experience the spiritual world directly, he compared this kind of sight to sunlight in winter, when everything is indeed clear but when nothing grows. I am mindful, incidentally, that the winter he was talking about was not that of twentieth-century Boston but of eighteenth-century Sweden.

As theologian, he saw the ideal as an intelligence totally mo-

tivated by love and, therefore, moved to act. This is the fulfillment of the whole person—heart, mind, and body—and not
the perfection of detached intellect.

This chapter does not begin to suggest the thoroughness
with which Swedenborg explored this theme. He loved detail
and had a holographic capacity for seeing universal principles
come to intense focus in minutiae. I hope the following selec-
tions do make it clear, however, that he saw "knowing" as a
wonderfully human enterprise, as a lifelong journey full of un-
certainty, full of companionship, and essentially focused on
values.

The Primacy of Affect

[There are things] that can be known, and then understood, if
only the mind enjoys them; for pleasure brings light with it
because it stems from love. For people who love matters of divine and heavenly wisdom, a light shines from heaven, and
they have enlightenment.

Heaven and Hell 265*

People who are not involved in compassion have only an
outward kind of sight or a lower kind of view. There is no way
they can see higher things from this perspective—the higher
things seem to them like darkness.

Arcana Coelestia 4783:6

The warmth of life comes from pleasures of affections and
delights of perceptions and thoughts. Since every affection has
its own [intrinsic] pleasure, and every thought therefore its
own [intrinsic] charm, we can conclude where the good and
the true come from and what they are intrinsically.

For all of us, the good is what brings pleasure to our affection, and the true is what therefore brings delight to our
thinking. So we all label "good" whatever we feel as pleasant,

*As is customary in Swedenborgian studies, the numbers following titles
refer to paragraph numbers, which are uniform in all editions, rather than to
page numbers.

4

from the love of our intentionality; and we label "true" whatever we therefore perceive as delightful, from the wisdom of our ability to discern.

Divine Providence 195:2

All our pleasure, contentment, and happiness come from our ruling love, and agree with it. We call what we love pleasant because it feels pleasant. While we may also call pleasant something we think but do not love, this is not a life pleasure. For us, life pleasure is what is good, and life pain is what is evil.

New Jerusalem and Its Heavenly Doctrine 58

To have perceptiveness in spiritual matters, we need to be absorbed in an affection for what is true, an affection whose source is good, and we need a constant longing to know what is true. This brings enlightenment to our ability to discern, and when this ability is enlightened, we are granted the ability to see profoundly into the intrinsic nature of things.

Arcana Coelestia 5937:3

We can see clearly love's ability to accept suitable truths, and love's longing to unite them to itself, in people who have been brought into heaven. Even though they may have been simple folk in the world, they nevertheless come into angelic wisdom. . . when they are in the company of angels. This is because they have loved the true and the good for the sake of the true and the good and have rooted them in their lives. . . .

Heaven and Hell 18

The reason love without discernment (or an affection of love without the thinking of discernment) can neither sense nor act in the body is that love without discernment is effectively blind, or an affection without thinking is effectively in the dark, since discernment is the light by which love sees. . . . All perception of the true comes from love within discernment, . . . and all the physical senses get their perceptiveness from the perceptiveness of their mind.

Divine Love and Wisdom 406

5

[P]leasure and charm in the mind are spiritual, while in the body they are natural. The two together constitute human life. We can see from this what it is for us that we call good and what it is that we call true; and we also can see what it is for us that we call evil and what we call false. Things are evil for us if they destroy the pleasure of an affection and false if they destroy the charm of our consequent thought. We can also see that the evil, from its pleasure, and the false, from its charm, can be called and believed to be good and true. In fact, the good and the true are changes and variations in the state of the mind's forms, but they are perceived and live only through their pleasures and charms.

Divine Providence 195:3

It needs to be realized that insights and truths are things no more removed from the purest substances (which belong to the inner person or spirit) than sight is removed from its organ, the eye, or hearing from its organ, the ear. There are purer substances, real substances, from which insights and truths arise, substances whose changes in form, enlivened and modified by an inflow of life from the Lord, present these phenomena; and it is their intersections and harmonies, sequential or simultaneous, that move us and that constitute what we call beautiful, charming, and pleasant.

Arcana Coelestia 3726:3

The Outreach of Thought

It is worth knowing what heaven's form is like, because not only are all [angels] associated according to it, all communication also occurs according to it; and since all communication occurs in this manner, so too does all the outreach of thoughts and affections, and likewise all the intelligence and wisdom of angels. This is why the extent to which someone is in the form of heaven—is, therefore, a form of heaven—determines how wise he or she is.

Heaven and Hell 201

6

To the extent that we are in the form of heaven,. . . we are involved in intelligence and wisdom. In fact,. . . all the think-ing of our discernment and all the affection of our intentional-ity reach out into heaven on all sides, according to its form, and communicate marvelously with the communities there, and they with us.

There are people who believe that thoughts and affections do not really reach out around them but occur within them, because they see their thought processes inside themselves and not as remote from them; but they are quite wrong. As eye-sight has an outreach to remote objects and is influenced by the pattern of things seen "out there," so too that inner sight that is discernment has an outreach in the spiritual world, even though we do not perceive it.

There was a spirit who believed that he thought indepen-dently—that is, without any outreach beyond himself and consequent communication with outside communities. To let him know that he was wrong, he was deprived of communica-tion with his neighboring communities. As a result, he not only lost [the power of] thought, he even collapsed, virtually lifeless—just able to flail his arms about like a newborn infant. After a while, the communication was restored to him, and bit by bit, as it was restored, he returned to his thinking state.

Heaven and Hell 203

The Nature of Perception

There are always two forces that are holding anything to-gether in its coherence and in its form—a force acting from the outside and a force acting from within. Where they meet is the thing that is being held together. This holds true for peo-ple, too, in respect to all their parts, even the most minute. It is recognized that there are atmospheres that, by their con-stant pressure or weight and consequent active force, are hold-ing the whole body together and also that air maintains the lungs by its inflow. Air also maintains the ear, with its inner forms constructed to respond to its changes. It is recognized that in like matter the ether effects a deeper coherence, since it flows freely through all our pores and keeps all our inner bodily organs in their coherent forms by a quite similar pressure or weight and consequent active force. This same atmosphere also maintains its organ, which is the eye, with its inner forms designed to respond to its changes.

When there is only a direct inflow from the Divine [which we could experience as arising from some unconscious level], the Lord is flowing in with what is good and true, but we are not conscious of it as good and true. . . . However, when there is at the same time an indirect inflow [i.e., through our environment], then the good is perceived because the indirect flow is into the outward, sensory level of our consciousness.

Arcana Coelestia 8701

[A]ll perception flows in through the inner [reaches of a person] into the outer or natural. The natural on its own perceives absolutely nothing. Its perception comes from something prior to itself; nor does the prior something perceive on its own, but from something still prior—ultimately then from the Lord, who exists on his own. The inflow is of this nature and, therefore, so is perception.

Arcana Coelestia 6040

The thinking of a healthy natural [mind: *cogitatio boni naturalis*] is the thinking of the rational or inner person within the natural or outer person, based on the good of that inner person. It is the rational or inner person who thinks, not the natural or outer, for. . . the inner person is in heaven's light, which has intelligence and wisdom within it, while the outer person is in the world's light, which has no intelligence in it, nor even any life. So if the inner person were not thinking within the outer, there would be no way for any thinking to occur. Yet our thinking does seem to us to occur in our outer person because we use for our thinking the things that come in through our senses and that belong to the [outside] world. In this respect, it is like our eyesight. Sense-oriented people think that the eye sees on its own. Yet the eye is only a physical organ through which the inner person sees things outside the body, in the world.

Arcana Coelestia 3679:2–3

Since the soul is spiritual substance, and by reason of order is more pure, more primary, and more inward, while the body is material and, therefore, more crude, more secondary, and more outward; and since it is in keeping with order for the more pure to flow into the more crude, the more primary into the more secondary, and the more inward into the more outward, it is, therefore, in keeping with order for the spiritual to flow into the material, and not the reverse. This means that the thinking mind flows into the sight, subject to the state imposed on the eyes by the things that are being seen—a state which that mind, further, organizes at will. In the same way, the perceiving mind flows into the hearing, subject to the state imposed on the ears by words.

Intercourse between the Soul and the Body 1

Insight from above into what is below (or from the more inward into the more outward, which is the same thing) is called inflow, since it occurs by means of an inflow. For example, if our more inward sight were not constantly flowing into our outer or eyesight, this latter could never apprehend or discern any object. For it is the more inward sight that apprehends through the eye what the eye is seeing: it is by no means the eye [that does this], even though it may seem so. We can also determine from this how involved people are in sensory illusions if they believe that their eye sees when, on the contrary it is the sight of their spirit, a more inward sight, that sees through the eye. . . .

But the same holds true also for this more inward or spiritual sight. This does not see on its own but from something still deeper, which belongs to its rational functioning. Even this does not see on its own but from something still deeper, which is the inner person. . . ; and ultimately it is not this but the Lord through the inner person who sees. He alone sees because he alone is alive and gives us both the ability to see and the appearance that we are seeing on our own. That is how the inflow works.

Arcana Coelestia 1954

Appearances

It needs to be realized that no truths are ever pure for us or even for angels—pure meaning devoid of appearances. They are all appearances, each and every one; and yet the Lord accepts them as truths if there is something good within them. Pure truths belong to the Lord alone because they are divine. The Lord is, so to speak, the good itself and the true itself.

Arcana Coelestia 3207:3

Truth adapted to angels is largely incomprehensible to people. . . . This is because angels talk about spiritual matters, which are removed from natural ones and, therefore, alien to the concepts and words of human speech. People have formed their concepts on the basis of things they have seen in the world and on the earth and have consciously touched, which things are material. The concepts of deeper human thought, even though they are supranatural, still find their definition in material things; and where they find their definition, there they seem to be. There we perceive what we are thinking.

Arcana Coelestia 7381:2

The intrinsic Divine is infinite, and the infinite cannot be united to finite things,. . . except by donning something finite and so by adapting itself for acceptance.

Arcana Coelestia 8760:2

All the misconceptions that are prevalent among evil people and among simple folk originate in "confirmed appearances." As long as appearances remain simply appearances, they are apparent truths, and it is all right for anyone to think and talk in terms of them. But once they are accepted as actual truths (which happens when they are confirmed), then these apparent truths become falsities and misconceptions.

For example, it is an appearance that the sun travels around the earth once a day and traces its ecliptic path once a year. As long as this is not confirmed, it is an apparent truth, and it is all right to think and talk in such terms. . . . However, when people make up their minds that this appearance is the actual truth, then they are thinking and speaking falsity as a result of misconception.

The same holds true for countless other appearances—not just in natural, civic, and moral matters, but even in spiritual ones.

Divine Love and Wisdom 108

Perception by Contrast

There is nothing in the universe that does not have its opposite; and opposites are not relative to each other but are contrary. There are relationships between the largest and the smallest instances of the same thing, but there are things contrary by opposition to them. These latter are relative to each other as the former are to each other, so the relationships themselves are opposites.

Marital Love 425

In addition to the spirit I have just been talking about, there were other spirits who argued the opposite case. . . . The people present knew just who these spirits were and what they were like, so they paid them no heed. Still, this is how they learn what is evil and what is good, since what is good is learned by means of what is evil; in fact, the quality of the good is recognized by its opposite. All perception of any reality depends on its reaction to boundaries [formed] from opposites of different kinds and degrees.

Arcana Coelestia 7812

We recognize the quality of the good only by its relationship to what is less good and by its opposition to what is evil. Our whole ability to perceive and to sense comes from this

11

source, since this is the source of its quality. . . . There must be variety in everything from its largest form to its smallest. When this variety occurs [also] in its opposite, from its smallest form to its largest, and when a balance is struck, then by degrees a relativity emerges; and perception and sensation of the thing either increases or decreases. It must be realized, though, that this opposition may either destroy or enhance perceptions and sensations. It destroys when [the opposites] mingle, and it enhances when they do not mingle.

Divine Providence 24

Temptation-trials [*tentationes*]. . . give the quality to our sensitivity to the good and the true, through the opposites that evil spirits then pour in. By our sensitivity to opposites, we acquire [a sense of] relationships, which is the source of all quality. In fact, no one knows what is good without knowing what is not good or knows what is true without knowing what is not true.

Arcana Coelestia 5356:2

Basic Assumptions

Spiritual truths cannot be grasped unless the following universal principles are known:

1. Everything in the universe goes back to the good and the true and to their mutual union in order to be anything. This means that everything goes back to love and faith and their union.

2. People have discernment and intentionality, discernment being the recipient vessel of the true and intentionality, the recipient vessel of the good. Everything in us goes back to these two and to their union, just as everything [in the universe] goes back to the true and the good and their union.

3. There is an inner and an outer person, as distinguishable from each other as heaven is from the world. Yet they need to make one if a person is to be truly human.

4. Heaven's light is the light the inner person is in, and the

world's light is the light the outer person is in. Heaven's light is the actual Divine-True that is the source of all intelligence.

5. There is a correspondence between the elements of the inner person and those of the outer. As a result, things from either side may appear in different guise, so different that they may not be recognized unless one is informed about correspondences.

Heaven and Hell 356e

I beg you, though, not to muddle your concepts with time and space. To the extent that there is time and space in your concepts as you read what follows, you will not understand it; for the Divine [the central topic Swedenborg is about to deal with] is not in time and space.

Divine Love and Wisdom 51

A knowledge of levels is like a key for unlocking the causes of things and entering into them. Without this knowledge, one can know hardly anything about the causes of things. In fact, the objects and subjects of each world seem straightforward, as though nothing more were involved than the eye can observe. Yet this, relative to what lies within, is only a minute fraction—most minute. The deeper matters that are not visible cannot be unveiled without a knowledge of levels. We progress from more outward to more inward things, and through these to the inmost, by levels—not by a continuous slope [literally, "continuous levels"] but by quantum leaps [literally, "discrete levels"].

Divine Love and Wisdom 184

We need to realize that how [truth] is applied depends on who is applying it. People involved in an affection for the true apply it to themselves according to their state and the quality of their affection. When people who are involved in an affection for the false apply it to themselves, they distort and falsify it. This enables us to determine that the Divine-True flows into everyone, but that it is [then] varied in individuals, depending on their state and the quality of their life.

Arcana Coelestia 7343

[T]he doctrines of the early church* taught about compassion and the neighbor. . . . But these teachings and facts have virtually disappeared now and have been replaced by doctrines of faith. If these are widowed or separated from doctrines of compassion, they teach almost nothing. For doctrines of compassion teach what is good, while doctrines of faith teach what is true. Teaching what is true without teaching what is good is like walking blind, since the good is what teaches and leads and the true is what is taught and led.

Arcana Coelestia 4844:4

Doubt, Reason, and Faith

Even though these things may seem paradoxical and unbelievable, they should still not be denied because experience itself commends them. If we were to deny everything whose causes we do not know, we would deny countless things that occur in nature—we know the causes of only a tiny fraction of them. . . .

Arcana Coelestia 4321

[N]o one should be instantly persuaded about the truth—that is, the truth should not be instantly so confirmed that there is no doubt left. The reason is that truth inculcated in this way is "second-hand" truth [*verum persuasivum*]—it has no stretch and no give. In the other life, this kind of truth is portrayed as hard, impervious to the good that would make it adaptable. This is why, as soon as something true is presented by open experience to good spirits in the other life, something opposite is presented soon thereafter, which creates a doubt. So they are enabled to think and ponder whether it is true and to gather reasons and thereby lead the truth into their minds

*In Swedenborg's view of the history of religion, there was an "earliest church" (*Ecclesia Antiquissima*) characterized by innocence and spiritual transparency. This declined and, at its nadir, was succeeded by an "early church (*Ecclesia Antiqua*) characterized by an understanding of and delight in the symbolic nature of physical reality.

14

rationally. This gives their spiritual sight an outreach in regard to this matter, even to its opposite.

Arcana Coelestia 7298:2

People who only argue whether [spiritual realities] exist remain outside the doors of wisdom, like people who only knock and cannot even peek into wisdom's splendid palaces. Strange as it is, people who do this consider themselves wiser than others, wiser to the extent that they can argue better. . . .

Arcana Coelestia 3428:3

[The highest angels] never reason about truth, much less argue whether it is so or not. They do not even know what "believing" or "having faith" are. "What is faith?" they say. "I see and perceive that this is true." They illustrate this with a comparison. It is as though someone with a friend were to see a house with various things in and around it and were to tell his friend that he ought to believe in the existence of these things, that they were what they seemed. Or it is as though someone were to see an orchard with its trees and fruits and tell his friend that he ought to have faith that it was an orchard and that those were trees and fruit when he could see them clearly with his own eyes.

Heaven and Hell 270:2

CHAPTER 2

Holistic Reality

·

It is obviously easier to manufacture definitions of reality than to agree on a single one. In his work *Quantum Reality* (1985), scientist Nick Herbert concludes that there are eight distinctly different possible definitions; but even so, there is no general agreement that his list is exhaustive. It may help to introduce some of Swedenborg's thoughts on the subject by a glance at the path he took in arriving at them.

As a young man studying science in England, Swedenborg was fascinated by the theories of Sir Isaac Newton, which were just becoming known. He would later take strong exception to Newton's concept of a vacuum; and on reflection, the reason seems clear: a vacuum places an absolute separation between any entities within it. Newton's laws indeed assume that the various particles, whether planets or pebbles, are absolutely discrete. It is an assumption that works marvelously well in the field of mechanics and that lies at the heart of much of our industrial technology.

However, since the work of Albert Einstein in particular, it has turned out that Newton's vacuum does not work very well at all on the cosmic scale or on the subatomic scale. In each of these realms, we need "wave concepts" as well as "particle concepts" to account for what we observe; and waves are remarkably "indiscrete"—they interact and overlap in ways that particles do not. The paradox of the one and the many that we find in early Greek philosophy is still with us, "the one" in the image of a single boundless field in which every electron is coextensive with the universe (as Pierre Teilhard de Chardin expressed it) and "the many" in the image of matter divisible into atoms that are divisible into smaller particles and, ultimately, into discrete quanta.

It should come as no surprise that an individual with extensive paranormal experience should stress the oneness of all that is. This is perhaps the most common and distinctive feature of mystical experience in all traditions. "Oneness" is a recurrent theme in Swedenborg's theological works, and his identification of the essence of that oneness as being a union of divine love and wisdom lays the groundwork for a profoundly ethical view of the cosmos and our place in it.

In the remarks prefaced to the first chapter, I singled out the concept of "distinguishable oneness" as pervasive and distinctive in Swedenborg's theological thought. It is nowhere more essential than in his view of the nature and relationship of love and wisdom, and much of what he has to say will be misunderstood unless it is remembered that, for him, there is no mental or intellectual "form" that does not have some affective or emotional "substance" and no intent or feeling that does not have some cognitive form. In later chapters, this will be seen as basic to his views of human nature, the human process of growth, and human relationships.

Equally remarkable, to my mind, are two further features of Swedenborg's thought in this regard. The first is that every entity is constituted by the intersection of two forces—by its direct connection with the Divine and by its involvement with its surroundings. This offers an inescapable "both/and" answer to the perennial nature/nurture debate and is wholly consistent with the rejection of absolute objectivity noted in the first chapter.

The second surprising feature is Swedenborg's explicit attention to wave phenomena. He does not use the words for "wave" (Latin: *unda, undare, undatio*) very often; but he does state that "influx" (a flowing-in) is a wave phenomenon, and the concept of "influx" is basic to his view of reality. This, in turn, gives a special twist to his view of the relationship between part and whole, which is surveyed in the final section of this chapter.

Once we leave the realm of mechanics and enter the realm of mind and spirit, we enter a domain that can only be described as holographic, with the Divine wholly present in every least part. It issues finally in a union of the cosmic and the personal in the principle that our individual acceptance into heaven depends on our acceptance of heaven into ourselves.

The One Ground of Being

If you gather everything that is known and subject it to your mental insight and explore in some elevation of spirit what is common to everything, you can only conclude that it is love and wisdom. These two are, in fact, the essentials of every aspect of a human life. Everything civil, everything moral, and everything spiritual depend on these two; and apart from them is nothing. The same holds true for the life of the aggregate person, . . . the larger or smaller community, the kingdom, the empire, the church, and the angelic heaven. Take love and wisdom away from them, and ponder whether they are anything, and you will arrive at the conclusion that, without these as their source, they are nothing.

Divine Love and Wisdom 28

Where there is Reality [*Esse*], there is Presence [*Existere*]: neither occurs apart from the other. Reality actually exists through Presence and not apart from it. . . . They are distinguishably one, like love and wisdom. Love, further, is Reality, and wisdom is Presence, since love occurs only in wisdom and wisdom, only from love. So, when love is in wisdom, it then has presence. These two are one in such a way that they can be distinguished in thought but not in fact; and since they can be distinguished in thought and not in fact, we, therefore, refer to them as "distinguishably one."

Divine Love and Wisdom 14

The common human notion of love and wisdom is of something volatile that flows in a subtle atmosphere or ether or of
something exhaled by something like this. Hardly anyone
thinks that they are, really and in fact, substance and form.
People who do see that they are substance and form still envi-
sion love and wisdom as outside their subject and flowing
from it, . . . not realizing that love and wisdom are the actual
subject and that what is seen outside it as volatile and flowing
is only the appearance of the states of the intrinsic subject.

Divine Love and Wisdom 40

The actual divine essence is love and wisdom.

Divine Love and Wisdom 28

Everything in the universe is a recipient of divine love and
divine wisdom. . . .

Divine Love and Wisdom 55

The Divine fills all space of the universe without [being
bound by] space.

Divine Love and Wisdom 69

The Divine is in all time without [being bound by] time.

Divine Love and Wisdom 73

The Divine is the same in the largest and the smallest
things. This follows from the two preceding sections, on the
Divine being in all space but not bound by space and in all
time but not bound by time. . . .

It does seem as though the Divine were not the same in one
person as in another—that it were different, for example, in a
wise person than in a simple one, different in an elderly person
than in an infant. But this appearance is deceptive. The person
is a recipient, and the recipient or recipient vessel may vary. A
wise person is a recipient of divine love and divine wisdom
more aptly and, therefore, more fully than a simple person and
an elderly person who is also wise, more than an infant or child.
Still, the Divine is the same in the one as it is in the other. . . .

The Divine is also the same in the largest and smallest of all created things that are not alive. . . .

Banish space—and absolutely rule out a vacuum—and then think about divine love and wisdom as actual essence once space is denied and vacuum ruled out. Then, think spatially, and you will perceive that the Divine is the same in the largest and the smallest [segments] of space.

Divine Love and Wisdom 77–81

Intersective Reality

It is recognized that, in every event [*operatione*], there is something active and something passive and that nothing happens from an active [force] alone or from a passive [force] alone.

Intercourse between the Soul and the Body 11

That [spiritual] sun, or divine love, cannot use its warmth and light to create anything directly from itself. In that case, the created entity would be love in its essence, which is the Lord. But it can create out of substances and materials so formed that they can receive that actual warmth and actual light. It is rather like the sun of our world, which cannot use its warmth and light directly to produce vegetation in the earth but uses substances of the soil that it can be in through its warmth and light, and thereby causes vegetation.

Divine Love and Wisdom 5

Unless there were matching forces reacting against these external forces and thereby holding together and stabilizing intermediate forms, these forms would not last a moment. So we can see that there must of necessity be two forces if anything is to arise and endure. The forces that flow in and act from within come from heaven, and through heaven from the Lord, and have life within them.

Arcana Coelestia 3628:2–3

20

Absolutely everything comes from the first Reality [*Esse*], and the design is so established that the first Reality is present in the derived forms [both] directly and indirectly, just as much in the most remote part of the design, therefore, as in its first part. The actual Divine-True is the only substance; its derivatives are simply successive secondary forms. This also enables us to see that the Divine does flow directly into absolutely everything. . . .

Arcana Coelestia 7004:2

[T]he Lord unites all the heavens by means of a direct and an indirect inflow—by a direct inflow from himself into all the heavens and by an indirect inflow from one heaven into another.

Heaven and Hell 37

Further, in regard to the union of heaven with the human race, it should be realized that the Lord himself flows into every individual according to heaven's design—into the individual's most inward and most outward [aspects] alike. . . . This inflow of the Lord is called direct inflow, while the other inflow, which happens by means of spirits, is called indirect inflow. . . . This divine inflow is constant and is accepted in the good in good people, but not in evil ones. These latter either reject it, stifle it, or corrupt it.

Heaven and Hell 297

Wave Motion

Since I have been in the company of spirits and angels constantly for nine years now, I have very carefully observed what inflow is like. When I thought, I could see solid concepts of thought as though they were surrounded by a kind of wave; and I noticed that this wave was nothing other than the kinds of thing associated with the matter in my memory and that, in this way, spirits could see the full thought. But nothing reaches [normal] human sensation except what is in the middle and seems to be solid. I have compared this surrounding wave to spiritual wings by which the object of thought is lifted out of the memory. This is what brings it to our attention.

I was able to determine that there was a great deal of associated matter in that surrounding wave-substance from the fact that spirits in a subtler sphere knew from it all I had ever known about the subject, drawing out and absorbing in this way everything proper to a person. The genii who are sensitive only to desires and affections draw out things proper to one's loves. For example, when I was thinking about someone I knew, then his image appeared in the middle as he looked when he was named in human presence; but all around, like something flowing in waves, was everything I had known and thought about him from boyhood. So that whole man, as he existed in my thought and affection, was instantly visible among the spirits. Again, when I thought about a particular city, then the spirits knew instantly from the surrounding sphere of waves everything I had seen and knew. The same holds true for matters of knowledge.

Arcana Coelestia   6200

I have also heard the speech of many spirits at once, undulating like a scroll. . . .

Arcana Coelestia   1763

[In heaven,] no one can pronounce a trinity of persons each of whom separately is God]—the heavenly aura itself, in which their thoughts fly and undulate the way sound does in our air, resists [such a pronouncement].

True Christian Religion   173:2

When a natural mind is acting out of the pleasures of its own love and the comfort of its own thinking (which are intrinsically evil and false), then the reaction of that natural mind sets aside the things proper to its spiritual mind. It blocks the doorway against their entry, it works things so that the source of behavior lies in the kinds of thing that agree with

22

its own reaction. This causes an action and reaction of the natural mind, opposed to the action and reaction of its spiritual mind. This results in a closing of the spiritual mind like a spiral twisting backwards.

If, however, the spiritual mind is opened, then the action and reaction of the natural mind are reversed. In fact, the spiritual mind is then acting from above or within, using all the while the elements within the natural mind that have been arranged in submission to it, from the more inward to the more outward. It retwists the spiral that the action and reaction of the natural mind are in. Actually, this latter mind is from birth in opposition to the characteristics of its spiritual mind. It derives this genetically from its parents, as is known.

This is what that change of state is like that we call reformation and regeneration. We may liken the state of a natural mind before reformation to a spiral twisting and bending itself around downwards, while, after reformation, we may liken it to a spiral twisting and bending itself around upwards.

Divine Love and Wisdom   263

Coherence

[N]othing unconnected over occurs, and anything unconnected would instantly perish.

Arcana Coelestia   2556

[N]othing occurs in all nature that does not somehow portray the Lord's kingdom in a general way. The natural [world] has its whole source in the spiritual kingdom. Anything lacking a prior source is nothing; nothing occurs that is not connected to a cause and, therefore, to a purpose. Anything unconnected would collapse instantly and become nothing.

Arcana Coelestia   2758

[T]here are connected stages from the First (that is, from the Lord) all the way to the last things, which are in humanity, and to the very last things, which are in nature. The last things in humanity, like those in nature, are relatively dark and, therefore, cold; and are relatively general and, therefore, hazy. We can see from this that, through these stages, there is a constant connection of all things with the First Reality. Inflow is patterned by these stages, for the Divine-True that emanates directly from the Divine-Good flows in by stages; and in its course, or at each new stage, it becomes more general and, therefore, coarser and hazier, and it becomes slower and, therefore, more viscous and colder. . . .

But we must be precisely aware that the Divine-True that flows into the third heaven (nearest the Lord) also flows without sequential adaptation into the last elements of the pattern, and from that First directly governs and oversees everything there. This is what holds the stages together in their pattern and coherence.

Arcana Coelestia 7270:3–4

The union of angelic communities into a single heaven rests in these laws.
1. Every unity in the heavens arises as a form of many elements joined together according to a heavenly concord.
2. Love is spiritual union, the source of heavenly concord.
3. There must be a universal bond if the specifics are to be kept united.
4. The universal bond flows into specific bonds and constitutes them.
5. The universal bond is the Lord: therefore, love from him and a consequent love for him.
6. The specific bonds are secondary and are mutual love or compassion toward the neighbor.

Arcana Coelestia 9613:3

Part and Whole

Before we say anything about the inflow and working of the soul into the body, it must be clearly recognized that the inner person is formed in the image of heaven and the outer in the

image of the world, even to the point that the inner person is a
heaven in miniature and the outer a world in miniature—a
microcosm.

Arcana Coelestia 6057

Heaven, if grasped as a single entity, reflects a single person.

Heaven and Hell 59

Each community in the heavens reflects a single person.

Heaven and Hell 68

Each angel is, therefore, in a perfect human form.

Heaven and Hell 78

I should like to offer a particular arcanum, hitherto unknown to anyone: namely, that everything good and true that
emanates from the Lord and makes heaven is in human form.
This holds true not only overall and on the grand scale but in
every part and in the smallest details. Further, this form influences everyone who accepts the good and the true from the
Lord and is why everyone in heaven is in human form depending on his or her acceptance.

This is why heaven is "like itself" in its larger and smaller
constituents and why the human form is the form of the
whole, of each community, and of each angel. . . . We should
also add to this that it is the form of the details of thought
from heavenly love within angels.

Heaven and Hell 460

Further, heaven as a whole is of such nature that each individual is like a center of all. In consequence, an image of
heaven is reflected in each individual and makes that individual
like itself—that is, a person. The nature of the inclusive whole,
in fact, determines the nature of the part of the whole since
the parts must be like their whole in order to belong to it.

Arcana Coelestia 3633

To the extent that anyone is in the form of heaven, he or
she is in heaven; in fact, he or she is a heaven in miniature.

Heaven and Hell 203

The universe in its greatest and smallest parts, in its first and its last forms, is so full of divine love and divine wisdom that we could say it is divine love and divine wisdom in image. . . . The created universe is an image that portrays the God-Man, and . . . his love and wisdom are . . . presented in the universe in an image.

Divine Love and Wisdom 52

Every created thing . . . is by nature recipient of God . . . : it is suitable because it was created in God by God; and because it was created in this way, it is an analogue and . . . is like an image of God in a mirror.

Divine Love and Wisdom 56

If only [people] knew that we are all born for heaven—accepted if we accept heaven into ourselves in the world and shut out if we do not.

Heaven and Hell 420

CHAPTER 3

Alternate Realities

.

Here we come to what may be the most controversial and, at the same time, a most essential feature of Swedenborg's thought—his insistence that "spirit" is in its own way just as solid and substantial as matter. Perhaps we should regard him as driven to this conclusion by his own devotion to empiricism and remember that the subtitle of his most popular work, *Heaven and Hell*, is "From Things Heard and Seen." He had come to trust his "spiritual senses" in the same disciplined way he had trusted his physical senses in his labors as a metallurgist and as a anatomist.

In the material he drafted before publishing his *Arcana Coelestia*, there is evidence of indecision about what to do with accounts of his experiences. He knew, on the one hand, that to publish them would be to open floodgates of skepticism, but he could scarcely suppress what was so basic to his own conviction—"I have seen, I have heard, I have felt" (*Arcana Coelestia* 68).

In this presentation, I have chosen to deal first with Swedenborg's rebuttal of the principle of "creation from nothing," Christian theology's usual way of avoiding pantheism. To him, creation from nothing was virtually indistinguishable from Newton's "vacuum," creating a discontinuity so radical that there could be no connection; and for him, anything disconnected from the only source of being would instantly perish. Creation must be both distinguishable from its creator and united to its creator— "distinguishably one."

Swedenborg describes, again on the basis of experience, distinct levels of reality, successively more distant from the

27

Divine and, therefore, reflecting it more dimly and ambiguously. Each level is directly dependent on the one immediately prior (or higher or more inward—spatial and temporal images are no more than "appearances of truth"), the most accessible example for us being the way in which our nonmaterial intentions and thoughts give rise to material actions and words, with those actions and words persistently too slow and crude to convey the swiftness and subtlety of our inner processes.

In sharp distinction from many gnostic constructions of reality, though, in which spheres are multiplied in what seems rather arbitrary fashion, Swedenborg's levels of spiritual reality are simple and coherent. The highest of human levels of spirituality he refers to as "the heavenly" (or "celestial" from the Latin *coeleste*): it is the state in which people are led spontaneously and unhesitatingly by their love of their God and of the neighbor. The second level he refers to as "the spiritual," the state in which people are led by their delight in first understanding and then doing the divine will. The third level, "the natural," is for people who are simply down-to-earth "doers," more interested in what works than in why it works. This arrangement is a kind of macrocosm of our individual trine of will, thought, and act; and a microcosm, in turn, of the divine trinity of love, wisdom, and providence.

This is directly relevant to our own present lives, in that we are from the very beginning residents, albeit unconscious ones, of the spiritual world. The spiritual world is not a place to which we go only after death but the environment of our present inner lives. If it were not for our "immersion" in material concerns, we would be far more conscious of this spiritual environment than we are. Swedenborg sees us as living spiritually in a realm between heaven and hell, with our daily choices moving us closer to one or the other. Death, by making us incapable of consciousness of this world, opens us to consciousness of the other; and after more or less sorting it out, we gravitate of our own accord to the kind of company we have come to prefer.

Heaven, as already suggested, is the all-inclusive community

of "the good"—of people who care about each other, percep-
tively and actively. The heavenly life is active as opposed to
contemplative, and the basis of its bliss is that the joy of each is
felt by all and the joy of all, by each. Hell, in contrast, is the
community of individuals who are utterly devoted to their
own interests, and its torment is a frustration based in the fact
that the satisfaction of one individual's desires is intolerable to
others, which means there cannot be two contented individuals in the same place at the same time. Hell is the ultimate
zero-sum game.

Distinct Levels of Reality

People say that the world as a whole was created from nothing, and they cherish a concept of nothing as really nothing at
all. Yet from "nothing at all," nothing is made and nothing
can be made. This is an abiding truth.

So the universe, which is an image of God and, therefore,
full of God, could not have been created except in God and
from God. God is, in fact, its actual reality, and it must be
what it is from its reality. . . .But even though it has been created in God and from God, it is not continuous from him. For
God is intrinsic reality, and there is no intrinsic reality in created things. If there were intrinsic reality in created things,
they would be continuous from God, and anything continuous from God is God.

Divine Love and Wisdom 55

Absolutely everything that comes into being in the spiritual
world and in the material world arises from distinct and gradient levels coinciding.

Divine Love and Wisdom 185

We use the term "gradient levels" to refer to losses or decreases—coarser to finer or denser to thinner—or better yet,
to additions or increases—finer to coarser or thinner to
denser—like levels of light progressing to darkness or levels of
warmth progressing to cold.

29

Distinct levels, though, are quite different. They are like earlier, later, and last things, like purpose, means, and result. We call these "distinct levels" because the earlier entity exists in its own right, the later in its own right, and the last in its own right; and yet if they are taken together, they constitute a single entity.

Divine Love and Wisdom 184

Further, unless these levels are recognized, one cannot know anything about distinctions in the more inward faculties of mind in people on earth or, therefore, anything about their state in terms of reformation and regeneration. Nor can one know anything about distinctions within the more outward faculties that pertain to the bodies of angels and of people on earth alike. And one can know absolutely nothing about the distinction between what is spiritual and what is natural and nothing, therefore, about the distinction of life between humans and animals or the distinction between more and less perfect animals or the distinction between the forms of the vegetable kingdom and the substances of the mineral kingdom.

Divine Love and Wisdom 185

For a better grasp of the nature and quality of distinct levels and the difference between them and continuous levels, let us use the angelic heaven as an illustration.

There are three heavens, and they are marked off by vertical levels. This means that one heaven is underneath another. They communicate only by an inflow that comes from the Lord alone through the heavens in proper sequence to the lowest heaven, not the other way around.

But each heaven is itself marked off not by vertical levels but by horizontal ones. People in the middle or at the center are in wisdom's light, while people who are at the circumference or at the boundaries are in wisdom's shadow. So, wisdom declines into ignorance the way light declines into shadow—along a continuum.

It is the same with people on earth. The more inward realms of their minds are marked off into the same number of levels as is the angelic heaven, with one level above another. So the more inward realms of people's minds are marked off by distinct or vertical levels. This is why individuals can be involved in their lowest level or a higher level or their highest level, depending on the level of their wisdom. This is why, when they are involved in their lowest level only, the higher level is closed and why this latter is opened as they accept wisdom from the Lord.

There are also continuous or horizontal levels in people on earth, just as there are in the heavens. The reason for the similarity between an individual and the heavens is that individuals are heavens in miniature, as far as the more inward realms of their minds are concerned, to the extent that they are involved in love and in wisdom from the Lord. On our being heavens in miniature as far as the more inward elements of our minds are concerned, see nn. 51–58 in the book *Heaven and Hell*.

Divine Love and Wisdom 186

Distinct levels relate to each other like thought and speech or like affection and behavior or like a feeling of the mind and an expression of the face. . . .

Last Judgment 307

That which works more inwardly is vastly stronger than that which works more outwardly, since the more inward, being purer, acts into the very particular details of the more outward and thus arranges the outward to suit itself. However, there must be something good and true in the outward in which the inflow from within can become concrete. . . .

Arcana Coelestia 6724

Our own more inward elements can be distinguished into levels and have boundaries at each level by which they are kept separate from the next lower level, from the most inward to the most outward. The first level is the more inward rational. Heavenly angels are in this level, or this is where the inmost or third heaven is. The second level is the more outward rational. Spiritual angels are in this level, or this is where the intermediate or second heaven is. The third level is the more inward

31

natural. Good spirits are in this level, or the lowest or first heaven. The fourth level is the more outward natural or sensory. This is where we are.

These levels within us are quite distinct. This is why we are miniature heavens inwardly if we live well or why our more inward reaches correspond to the three heavens. This is also why, after death, if we have lived lives of compassion and love, we can be brought into the third heaven. But for this situation to obtain, it is necessary that all the levels be well bounded and distinguished from each other by these boundaries. When they are bounded or distinguished from each other by these boundaries, then each level is a plane in which things come to rest, where the good that is flowing in from the Lord is accepted. Without these [boundaries] as planes, the good is not accepted but flows through, as though through a sieve or a perforated basket, all the way to the sensory; and there, having had no guidance in its course, it turns into filth.

Arcana Coelestia 5145:2–3

If the reader does not know that levels exist, does not know what they are and what their nature is, what follows will be incomprehensible, since there are levels within every created thing and, therefore, in every form. So in this part of the present work, we must discuss levels.

We can establish clearly the existence of levels of love and wisdom through angels of the three heavens. Angels of the third heaven so surpass angels of the second heaven in love and wisdom, and these latter so surpass angels of the lowest heaven, that they cannot live together. The levels of love and wisdom distinguish and separate them.

This is why angels of lower heavens cannot climb up to angels of higher heavens; and if they are allowed to climb up, they do not see them or anything around them. The reason they do not see them is that the love and wisdom of the higher angels is on a higher level, which transcends their perception. Each individual angel actually is his or her love and his or her wisdom. Further, love united to wisdom is a person in its form because God, who is love itself and wisdom itself, is a person.

32

I have sometimes been allowed to see angels of the lowest heaven climb up to angels of the third heaven. And when they had arrived, I heard them complain that they did not see a single person, even though they were surrounded by them. Afterwards, they were taught that the higher angels had been invisible to them because their love and wisdom were beyond their perception and that love and wisdom make an angel look like a person.

We can see even more clearly that levels of love and wisdom occur if we compare angels' love and wisdom to human love and wisdom. It is recognized that angels' wisdom is indescribable by comparison. We shall see below that it is also incomprehensible to us as long as we are involved in natural love. The reason it seems indescribable and incomprehensible is that it is on a higher level.

Because there are levels of love and wisdom, there are levels of warmth and light as well. By warmth and light, we mean spiritual warmth and light—the kind angels have in the heavens and the kind we have in the more inward regions of our minds. For we have a warmth of love and light of wisdom like that of angels.

The situation in the heavens is like this. The amount and quality of angels' love determine the amount and quality of their warmth. Their light bears the same relationship to their wisdom. The reason is that, as already explained, love for them is within warmth and wisdom, within light.

The same holds true for people on earth; but there is the difference that angels feel this warmth and see this light, while we do not. This is because we are involved in natural warmth and light; and as long as we are, we feel spiritual warmth only through a kind of pleasant sensation of love and see spiritual light only through the perception of something true.

Divine Love and Wisdom   179–181

In sequential order, the first level is the highest and the third is the lowest; but in simultaneous order, the first level is the inmost and the third, the outmost.

Divine Love and Wisdom   205

The last level is the complex, the vessel, and the basis of the earlier levels.

Divine Love and Wisdom 209

The vertical levels are in their fullness and their power in the last level.

Divine Love and Wisdom 217

We can see what correspondence is like from a person's face. In a face that has not been taught to dissimulate, all the affections of the mind present themselves to view in a natural form as in their imprint. This is why the face is called the index of character, a spiritual world, therefore, within a natural world. In like manner matters of understanding are present within speech and matters of intentionality, in physical actions.

Heaven and Hell 91

The Presence of the Spiritual

We are so created as to be in the spiritual world and in the natural world at the same time. The spiritual world is where angels are, and the natural world is where mortals are. And since we are created in this way, we have been given an internal and an external—an internal through our involvement in the spiritual world and an external through our involvement in the natural world. Our internal is what is called the inner person, and our external is what is called the outer person.

New Jerusalem and Its Heavenly Doctrine 36

We have been so created by the Lord that we might, while living in the body, have been able to talk with spirits and angels as they did in the earliest times; for we are one with them, being spirits clothed with bodies. But since, with the passage of time, we have so immersed ourselves in physical and worldly concerns that scarcely anything else matters to us, the way has been closed. Still, the moment the physical things we

are immersed in fade away, the way is opened; we are among
spirits and are living in their company.

Arcana Coelestia 69

Now, since each and every thing in the world and its nature
emerges and keeps emerging (that is, persists) from things
prior to itself, it follows that things emerge and persist from a
world that is above nature, which is called the spiritual world.
And since there must be a constant connection in order for
things to persist or keep emerging, it follows that the purer or
more inward things in nature and, therefore, in human beings
are from this source. It also follows that these purer things or
more inward things are so formed that they can accept an inflow.

Arcana Coelestia 4524

Everything in a person—both in the outer person and in the
inner—has a correspondence with the universal human. Apart
from a correspondence with this human (that is, with heaven,
or with the spiritual world, which amounts to the same thing),
nothing whatever emerges or persists. This is because it would
have no connection with the First, that is, with the Lord.
Whatever is not connected—and is, therefore, not dependent—cannot last for a moment. Its enduring stems from its
connection and dependence on that source from which all
emergence originates, for enduring is constant emergence.
This is why not only everything in a person is a correspondent,
so too is everything in the universe. . . . Everything we see
under the sun is a correspondent—every member of the animal kingdom and every member of the vegetable kingdom.
Each one, unless there were an inflow into it from the spiritual
world, would instantly collapse and disintegrate, as I have
been shown by an abundance of experience. . . .

Arcana Coelestia 5377

Holding to generalities, all things in a person who is truly
rational (that is, reborn) all affections, perceptions, and

35

thoughts are united with each other as though by blood relationship and kinship. They are, in fact, so arranged that they regard each other as families of a single household. . . . They derive this from the inflow of heaven, that is, of the Lord through heaven. In a person who is truly rational (that is, reborn), all things are arranged in the same order that prevails in heaven, which is the result of the inflow. This is the source of our ability to think, decide, evaluate, and reflect, an ability so marvelous that it eludes all human wisdom and science and defies any analyses that human diligence would extract from it. The reason these facts have not yet been recognized is that people do not believe that all affections, perceptions, and thoughts flow in, the evil ones from hell and the just ones from heaven—that is, that they have a connection with things beyond themselves. Yet the fact is that, as to our spirits, we are so united with those beyond us that, if we were denied this connection, we would not live for an instant.

Arcana Coelestia 2556

The reason people are unaware that mentally they are surrounded by spirits is that the spirits who are our companions in the spiritual world are thinking and talking spiritually, while, as long as we are in our bodies, we are thinking and speaking naturally. A natural person cannot understand or perceive spiritual thought and speech, or the reverse. This is why we cannot see spirits.

But once our spirits are in the company of spirits in their own world, then we are involved in spiritual thought and speech with them, because the human mind, while outwardly natural, is inwardly spiritual. So, through our more inward elements we communicate with spirits, while, with our more outward ones, we communicate with each other on earth. . . .

The spiritual world consists of heaven and hell. Heaven is overhead, and hell underneath. . . . They are not extended spatially but look as though they were. Between heaven and hell, there is a great interspace, which looks like a complete globe to the people who live there. . . .

Everyone is changing his or her location in that world from infancy to old age. As infants, we are kept in the eastern quarter toward the north. When as children we learn our first lessons about religion, we move gradually from the north toward the south. As we begin to think independently in adolescence, we are moved further south; and as we judge for ourselves and take charge of our own lives, we are moved into the southern quarter toward the east. This depends on our growth in matters that, seen inwardly, involve God and love for the neighbor. If we incline toward evil and absorb it, we move toward the west.

True Christian Religion 475

Death and Dying

I can solemnly avow that, as soon as we die, we are in the other life and are living as spirits among spirits. Further, we then look to ourselves and to others exactly like people in this world, furnished with every sense both inner and outer. Specifically, physical death is simply the loss of the things that served us for our usefulness and functioning in this world. First and foremost, death itself is a continuation of life but in another world, invisible to the eyes of our earthly bodies but visible there in a light that surpasses by a thousandfold the light of noonday on earth. Since I know this from so many years' first-hand experience right up to the present time, I can solemnly avow it. I now talk, and have talked in the past, with almost all the people I have known in the world who have died, with some just two or three days after their decease. Most of them were quite embarrassed that they had not believed that life would continue after death. I have talked with them not just for a day but over months and years, and I have been allowed to witness the successive states of their lives, moving either toward heaven or toward hell.

Arcana Coelestia 8939:2

Christians don't realize that heaven comes from the human race. They think heaven comes from angels who were created first of all and that hell comes from a devil or satan who was created angelic but rebelled and was cast down with his co-horts. . . .

[One] reason for this misunderstanding is the belief that no one will get to heaven or hell until after the last judgment. This involves the belief that everything visible will be demol-ished and then made new, that souls will then return to their bodies so that people live as people again. This goes together with the idea of angels as a separate creation, since you can't very well believe that heaven and hell come from the human race if you think that no one will get there until after the end of the world.

The Last Judgment 14–15.

I was once led into a state of unconsciousness as to my physical senses, thus nearly into the state of people who are dying, but with my inner life remaining intact and with the ability to think, so that I could grasp and retain in memory what happens to people who die and are awakened. . . .

Arcana Coelestia 169

When we cross from the natural world into the spiritual, which happens when we die, we take with us everything that is ours, everything personal, except our earthly bodies. This has been demonstrated to me by an abundance of experience. For when we enter the spiritual world or the life after death, we are in a body as we were in the world. There is no obvious dif-ference because we neither feel nor see any difference. But this body is spiritual, separated and purified from earthly things; and when the spiritual touches and sees the spiritual, it is just the same as when the natural touches and sees the natural.

Heaven and Hell 461

In regard to our sensory abilities right after death, it is like this. As soon as we die and our physical elements have cooled, we are awakened into that life and into a state then possessed of all our senses—so much so that at first we scarcely realize that we are not still in the body. The sensory abilities we possess actually lead us to believe this. But once we notice that we have more exquisite sensations, and especially when we begin to talk with other spirits, then we realize that we are in another life and that our physical death was a continuation of the life of our spirit.

Arcana Coelestia 4622:4

Human wisdom, which is natural as long as we are living in this natural world, can never be raised into angelic wisdom but only into some likeness of it. The reason is that the raising of the natural mind takes place along a continuum, as from darkness to light or from coarser to finer. However, a person whose spiritual level has been opened comes into that wisdom at death and also can come into it by having physical sensations go to sleep and then by an inflow from above into the spiritual elements of his or her mind.

Divine Love and Wisdom 257:4

As long as we are living in this world, we have no knowledge of the opening of these levels within ourselves. This is because we are involved in the natural level, which is the lowest, and we are thinking, intending, speaking, and acting from this level. The spiritual level, which is more inward, does not communicate with the natural level along a continuum but through correspondences, and communication through correspondences is not sensed.

However, when we leave the natural level, which happens when we die, then we come into that level which has been opened within us in this world. If the spiritual level has been opened in us, then we arrive in the spiritual level; if the heavenly level has been opened in us, then we arrive in the heavenly level.

Divine Love and Wisdom 238

Angels and spirits, or people after death, can meet all the people they have known in the world and people they have heard of—anyone they wish. They can see them face-to-face and talk with them, when the Lord allows it. And, remarkably, they are instantly present. So it is possible to talk not only with one's friends, who are encountered quite often but also with others whom one has admired and respected.

Arcana Coelestia 1114

People who think from a strictly natural light cannot grasp the fact that anything in heaven would be like things on earth. This is because they have thought and decided from that light that angels are only minds and that minds are like airy vapors, so that they do not have the senses that mortals have—no eyes, therefore, and if their are no eyes, there are no objects [of vision]. Yet angels have all the senses mortals have, far more exquisite, in fact. . . . I cannot briefly describe how things look to angels in the heavens. For the most part, they are like things on our earth but more perfect in form and more abundant in number. . . . But though the things one sees in heaven are largely similar to things on earth, they are not alike in essence. . . . The things in the heavens do not arise the way things on earth arise. In the heavens, everything comes from the Lord in correspondence with the more inward natures of the angels. . . . Since everything that corresponds to more inward things also portrays them, they are called portrayals; and since they vary depending on the state of the more inward natures of the people there, they are called *appearances*. Still, the things visible to angels' eyes in the heavens and perceived by their senses are as really visible and perceptible as things on earth are to us much clearer, in fact, crisper and more convincing. Appearances from this source in the heavens are called *real appearances* because they really happen. There are also appearances that are not real, things that are sometimes seen but do not correspond to more inward things. We will discuss these later.

Heaven and Hell 170–173; 175

The World of Spirits

The world of spirits is neither heaven nor hell; it is a place or state midway between the two. There, we first arrive after death; and, from there, we are, after a while, either raised into heaven or cast into hell, depending on our lives.

The world of spirits is a place midway between heaven and hell and also our intermediate state after death. I have been able to see that it is an intermediate place because the hells are below it and the heavens above. I have been able to see that it is an intermediate state because, as long as we are there, we are neither in heaven nor in hell. A state of heaven in us is the union of the good and the true in us, and a state of hell is the union of the evil and the false in us.

Heaven and Hell 421—422

People can know, if only they use their reason, that the life we acquire in this world follows us: that is, we are involved in the same kind of life after death. They can, in fact, know that no one can shed the life acquired from infancy without dying utterly and that this life cannot be instantly changed into something else, much less its opposite. For example, if some- one has acquired a life of deceit and finds the delight of life in it, then that individual cannot shed a life of deceit but remains involved in it after death as well. . . . Removing such things is impossible without extinguishing every trace of life.

Arcana Coelestia 3957:3

We can see from the foregoing that a spiritual state is quite different from a natural one, since it is characteristic of a spiri- tual state that one cannot be anywhere but where one's ruling love is. This is, in fact, where the delight of life is, and every- one wants to be in his or her delight of life. The human spirit cannot be anywhere else because this constitutes its life, its very breathing and heartbeat.

It is different in the natural world. Here, the outward form of a person is trained from infancy to simulate in facial expres- sion, speech, and act delights other than those of the inner person. So we cannot draw conclusions from the human state in the natural world about our state after death. For our state after death is spiritual, which means that it is not possible to be anywhere but in the delight of the love we have acquired through our life in the natural world.

This makes it quite clear that no one can be admitted into heaven's delight (commonly called heavenly bliss) who is in the delight of hell. . . . This is even clearer from the fact that, after death, no one is prevented from climbing into heaven: he is shown the way, he is given the means, he is allowed in. But once this person enters heaven and is influenced by the breath of its joy, he begins to feel pain in the breast and agony in the heart and to feel faint, twisting like snakes placed near a fire. Turning away from heaven and toward hell, he dashes away headlong and finds no rest until he reaches a community of his own love.

Divine Providence 338:5, 6

We undergo three states after death, before entering either heaven or hell. The first state is a state of more outward things; the second is a state of more inward things; and the third is a state of preparation. We undergo these states in the world of spirits. . . .

As to the first state, the state of more outward things, we enter this immediately after death. We all have, as to our spirits, more outward and more inward aspects. The more outward aspects of spirit are the ones by which it adjusts the human body to [conditions] in the world, especially our face, speech, and actions, for getting along with other people. The more inward aspects of spirit are the matters of our actual intent and its consequent thought, which are rarely obvious in face, speech, or act. From infancy, we have accustomed ourselves to showing friendship, good will, and sincerity and concealing what our actual intent is thinking. So we habitually carry around a life that is civilly and morally acceptable, no matter what we are like inside. . . .

Our first state after death is like this state in the world because we are at that point similarly involved in external concerns. Face, speech, and personality are similar, and so, therefore, are moral and civil behavior. . . . So the one is carried over into the other, and death is only a crossing.

Heaven and Hell 491–493

Our second state after death is called a state of more inward things because we are then let into the deeper workings of our

minds or of our intentionality and thinking, and the more outward concerns we were involved in during the first state go to
sleep. . . .

When spirits are let into the state of their more inward
workings, then it can be clearly seen what kind of people they
were in the world because they are acting from their genuine
selves. People who were inwardly good in the world behave
rationally and wisely—more wisely than in the world, in fact,
because they have been freed from their connection with a
physical body and, therefore, from those earthly things that
darken and, so to speak, becloud. People who were inwardly
evil in the world, on the other hand, behave grossly and
crazily—more grossly and crazily than in the world, in fact,
because they are now in freedom and are not restrained. . . .
Hidden things are thus opened and secrets laid bare. . . .

Heaven and Hell 499

Every evil bears its own punishment with it: they are united.
So the person who is involved in an evil is also involved in the
punishment of that evil. Still, no one after death undergoes
punishment for evils done in the world but only for evils done
then and there. But it boils down to the same thing, . . . since
everyone returns to his or her own life after death and, therefore, returns to similar evils.

Heaven and Hell 509

Our third state after death, or the third state of our spirit, is
a state of instruction. This state is appropriate to people who
are entering heaven and becoming angels, but not for people
who are entering hell because these latter cannot be taught
anything. So, their second state is also their third and ends by
their turning completely toward their own love and, therefore,
toward the hellish community that is in the same love. . . . But
good people are brought through from the second state into a
third, which is a state of their preparation for heaven through
instruction. The only way anyone can be prepared for heaven
is by insights into what is good and true—therefore, only
through being taught. For no one can know what is spiritually

good and true and what is evil and false . . . without being taught.

Heaven and Hell 512

Teaching in the heavens is different from teaching on earth because insights are not committed to memory but to life since spirits' memory is in their life. They accept and absorb what agrees with their life and do not accept, much less absorb, what does not agree. For spirits are affections and are, therefore, in a human form like that of their affections. . . .

An affection for the truth suited to their use is instilled by various means, most of which are unknown in this world. The primary one is through portrayals of constructive services, which can be presented in the spiritual world in thousands of ways, with such delight and charm that they enter the spirit from the more inward reaches of the mind to the more outward reaches of the body and thereby affect the whole person. In this way, the spirit virtually becomes his or her use. As a result, when spirits arrive in their community, . . . they are in their life when they are involved in their use.

Heaven and Hell 517

Heaven

The angels, taken all together, are called heaven, because they constitute it. Still, it is the Divine emanating from the Lord that flows into angels and is accepted by them that constitutes heaven overall and in detail. The Divine emanating from the Lord is the good of love and the truth of faith; so to the extent that people accept the good and the true from the Lord, they are angels, and they are heaven.

Heaven and Hell 7

Heaven is granted only to people who know the way to it and who travel that way. This way can to some extent be known by recognizing what kind of people make up a heaven, and by recognizing that no one becomes an angel, or arrives in heaven, who does not bring along from this world something angelic. Inherent in this angelic something is a recognition of the way from having walked in it and a walking in the way from having recognized it. In the spiritual world, there really are ways that lead to each heavenly and each hellish community, and we all spontaneously see our own ways. The reason we see them is that there is a way for every love, and love opens it and leads us to our kindred spirits. No one sees any way but that of his or her own love.

Divine Providence 60

The reason angels are not superior to mortals but are simply their equals . . . is that all angels have once been people on earth, and none of them [was] directly created as angels. . . They do indeed surpass mortals in wisdom, but this is because they are in a spiritual state and are, therefore, in heaven's light and not in a natural state . . . the way we are on earth.

The Apocalypse Revealed 818

[A]ngelic and human minds are alike. They both enjoy the abilities to discern, perceive, and intend; and they are both formed for the acceptance of heaven. For the human mind is just as sensitive as the angelic mind. The reason it is not as sensitive in this world is that it is in an earthly body; and in an earthly body, a spiritual mind thinks naturally. But it is different when it has been freed from its bond with that body. Then it no longer thinks naturally but spiritually, and then it thinks things beyond the comprehension or expression of the natural person—it is, therefore, wise like an angel.

Heaven and Hell 314

I knew a man of indifferent learning in the world; and after his death, I saw him and talked with him in heaven. I grasped clearly that he talked like an angel and that the things he said were beyond the grasp of a natural person.

Divine Love and Wisdom 239

If you were to see [angels] as I have, you would be stunned. They are actually instances of heavenly love and compassion in form, which is the truly human form.

Arcana Coelestia 9503

[F]rom angels . . . so much love flows forth that you would think they are nothing but love. It flows from their whole body, so that their body seems radiant and clear because of the light that comes from it. . . .

Arcana Coelestia 6135:3

I have also been allowed to perceive, by an inflow, the sweetness of angels, which they sense from not thinking and intending from themselves but from the Lord. This yields them quietness, peace, and contentment.

Arcana Coelestia 6469

An angelic life consists in service and in the good of compassion. Angels find nothing more joyous than enlightening and teaching spirits arriving from this world; than helping people, controlling evil spirits so that they do not exceed their limits and instilling good into them; than awakening the dead into the life of eternity and, if possible, . . . leading them into heaven.

Arcana Coelestia 454

Heaven becomes more perfect as more people enter it. This is because its form, which governs all its societal patterns and communications, is the most perfect of all. In the most perfect form, "more members" means a more complete focusing and agreement, and, therefore, a more intimate and whole-hearted union. The agreement and union are strengthened by numbers because each new member comes in as a welcome intermediary between members already present. Each new arrival strengthens the fabric and joins others more closely.

The Last Judgment 12

Old age, in its inner meaning, does not mean old age because the inner person, or the human spirit, does not know what old age is. Rather, as the body or the outer person ages, the inner person makes a passage into a new life. The human spirit is perfected by age as its body declines. This is intensified in the other life: people there in heaven are being continually

brought by the Lord into a more perfect life and eventually
into the flower of youth, even people who die at a ripe old
age.

Arcana Coelestia 4676

Angels are not always in the same state as to love nor, therefore, in the same state as to wisdom, since all their wisdom is
from their love and depends on their love. Sometimes they are
in a state of intense love, sometimes in a state of less intense
love. It declines gradually from its greatest to its least. When
they are in the highest level of their love, then they are in the
light and warmth of their love or in its clarity and delight; but
when they are in its lowest level, then they are in shade and
cold or in darkness and discomfort. From this last state, they
return again to the first, and so on. The stages follow one after
another, never exactly the same. These states follow like the
changes of state of light and shade, warmth and cold, or like
morning, noon, evening, and night, the particular days in this
world, with a constant variety throughout the year. . . .

Heaven and Hell 155

I have been told from heaven why these changes occur.
Angels have said that there are several reasons. First, because
the delight of life and heaven they have from the love and wisdom the Lord gives them would gradually grow stale if they
were in it incessantly. . . . Second, because they have just as
much self-image [*proprium*] as we do, . . . and because everyone loves his or her self-image, these changes of state or successive stages occur. Third, because this is how they are perfected, since they get used to being kept in the Lord's love
and withheld from self-love.

Heaven and Hell 158

Since heaven is from the human race and since, therefore,
angels are of both sexes and since by creation woman is for
man and man for woman—each for the other—and since a
love of the other is innate in each, it follows that there are

47

marriages in heaven just as there are on earth; but the marriages in heaven are quite different from earthly ones. . . .
Marriage in the heavens is the uniting of two people into one
mind.

Heaven and Hell 366

It is the general opinion that people born outside the
church, the ones called "the nations" or "the Gentiles," cannot be saved because they do not have the Word and, therefore, do not know the Lord; and apart from the Lord, there is
no salvation. It could be realized that they are saved, though,
simply from the fact that the Lord's mercy is universal, meaning that it extends to every individual. . . .

People who know what makes heaven can know that Gentiles are saved just as Christians are. For heaven is within us,
and we enter heaven if we have heaven within us. Heaven in us
is to acknowledge the Divine and to be led by the Divine. . . .
It is recognized that Gentiles lead just as moral lives as Christians do many of them, more moral lives. . . . Anyone who
lives a moral life for the sake of the Divine is being led by the
Divine. . . .

Heaven and Hell 318–319

Hell

The relationship of heaven to hell and of hell to heaven is like
that between two opposite [forces] that are acting against each
other, from whose action and reaction there results a balance
in which all events take place. . . .

Heaven and Hell 536

The opinion prevails among some people that God turns his
face away from people, rejects them from himself, and casts
them into hell; and that he is angry against them because of
their evil. Some go even further and believe that God punishes
people and does them ill. People support this opinion from
the literal meaning of the Word, which does say things like
this, since they do not realize that the spiritual meaning of the

Word, which makes sense out of the literal meaning, is quite different. [This latter meaning] teaches that God never turns his face away from us, never rejects us from himself, never casts anyone into hell or is angry. . . .

[W]e do evil from hell, and we do good from the Lord. But since we believe that whatever we are doing we are doing on our own, the evil we do clings to us as ours. This is why we are responsible for our own evil, not the Lord. The evil we do is hell within us, for it makes no difference whether you say "evil" or "hell."

Now, since we are responsible for our own evil, we rather than the Lord lead ourselves into hell. . . . Our whole intentionality and love stays with us after death. If in this world we have intended and loved evil, we intend and love this same evil in the other life and no longer let ourselves be led away from it. This is why people who have been involved in evil are connected to hell and are actually there as to their spirits; and after death, they want nothing more than to be where their evil is.

Heaven and Hell 545; 547

I have been allowed to look into the hells and see what they are like inside. . . . Some of the hells looked like caves or underground chambers; . . . some, like the dens or lairs of wild beasts in the forest; . . . some, like the vaulted chambers and crypts we find in mines. . . . In some hells, there seem to be the ruins of houses or of cities after a fire, where hellish spirits live and hide out. In the milder hells, there are buildings like crude huts, in places gathered into a neighborhood with lanes and streets. In these houses are hellish souls, quarreling angrily, beating and stabbing each other. There are robberies and muggings in the streets. . . . There are also dark forests where hellish souls roam like wild animals, with caves where they hide if others chase them. Then, too, there are desert areas where everything is sterile and sandy, with here and there irregular rocks riddled with caves. . . .

Heaven and Hell 586

All the spirits in the hells, seen in some touch of heaven's light, seem to be forms of their evil. Each is, in fact, an image of his or her evil, since everyone's more inward and more outward aspects are acting in harmony and the more inward things are presented to view in the more outward, which are the face, the body, speech, and behavior. . . . In general terms, they are forms of contempt for others, of threats against people who do not show them respect. They are forms of various kinds of hatred; they are forms of vindictiveness of various sorts. Savagery and cruelty show through from within; though when other people praise or respect or revere them, their faces compose themselves and seem happy. . . .

Heaven and Hell   553

CHAPTER 4

The Human Form

.

The reality of spirit treated in general terms in the last chapter is characteristic of each individual as well. Our thoughts and feelings seem shadowy and insubstantial to us because our physical senses dominate our consciousness; but from a spiritual point of view, it is matter that is fleeting and spirit that is enduring. Our physical appearance may have little to do with our actual character, and it is our actual character that matters supremely and forever.

The "distinguishable oneness" of love and wisdom is reflected in our own natures. For Swedenborg, the essence of being human consists of freedom, which is a matter of love, and rationality, which is a matter of wisdom. Our love is to our wisdom as substance is to form—distinguishable but inseparable—and it is the substance more than the form that determines our fundamental quality or character. Further, there is a hierarchical structure to our loves, with the basic ones finding expression is specific aims. Swedenborg would have had no trouble at all recognizing the phenomenon we refer to as a "hidden agenda." "What we love above all things is inside our purposing like the hidden current of a river," he wrote in *Arcana Coelestia* 8855.

In fact, the same levels that characterize the spiritual world are seen as characteristic of us as individuals. All, including self-love, are good when the higher rule the lower. Evil enters the picture only as the lower levels begin to rule the higher. Equally significant, there is nothing outside us in the natural or the spiritual world that does not have its equivalent within

51

us. We are microcosms; and as we come to recognize this, self-understanding, mutual understanding, and understanding of the world around us engage and enrich each other.

Ideally, then, we are at home in our God's creation—temporarily at home in this world and profoundly at home in the spiritual world, which vividly reflects our own deepest nature.

General Considerations

[W]e are all spirits inwardly; this is what is alive in the body, and not the body on its own. It is our spirit from which our body gets its human form—our spirit, therefore, that is primarily human. Further, it has a similar form, invisible to our physical eyes but visible to the eyes of spirits.

Arcana Coelestia 10758:3

The soul is the human form, from which nothing whatever can be taken away, to which nothing whatever can be added; and it is the inmost form of all the forms of the whole body. And since the forms outside it get their essence and their form from inmost things, [people] are . . . souls. In a word, the soul is the essential person because it is the inmost person: its form is, therefore, fully and perfectly the human form. Still, it is not life but is the nearest recipient vessel of the life that comes from God. . . .

Marital Love 315:11

A human being is an organ of life, and God alone is life. God pours his life into the organ and all its parts, as the sun pours its warmth into a tree and all its parts. Further, God grants people a sense that the life in them seems to be their own. God wants us to have this sense, so that we may live in apparent independence, according to the laws of the [divine] design . . . and may thus dispose ourselves to accept the love of God. Yet God continually keeps his finger on the vertical tongue of the balance, so to speak, to keep it within bounds. Still, he never violates our free choice by compulsion. . . . Our

52

free choice results from the fact that we have a sense that the
life we enjoy belongs to us.

True Christian Religion   504:5

Since these [spiritual] forms or substances are not visible to
the physical eye, people today have only the notion that insights and thoughts are abstract things. This is the source of
the insanity of our century, that people do not believe they
have a spirit within them that is going to live after their physical death, when, in fact, this [spirit] is a much more real substance than the material substance of their body.

Arcana Coelestia   3726:4

We have stated . . . in many places that the spirit is the inner
part of a person and the body, the outer. People who do not
grasp the relationship between the human spirit and the
human body may gather from this that the spirit lives inside
the body and that the body somehow surrounds and clothes it.
It needs to be realized, though, that the human spirit is in the
body—in all of it and in every part—and that it is the body's
purer substance, both in its motor organs and in its sensory organs and everywhere else, and that the body is a material entity
connected to it at every point, suited to the world in which it
exists. This is what we mean by saying that the spirit is the person and that the body serves it for uses in this world and that
the spirit is the inner part of a person and the body, the outer.

Arcana Coelestia   4659

Human Substance and Human Form

There are countless substances and forms in the human brain
where all our inner sensation dwells, everything involved in
our discerning and intending. However, . . . all our affections,
perceptions, and thoughts are not some kind of emanation
from these substances but are actual, real subjects that do not
give anything off but rather undergo changes in response to
stimuli from the outside.

Divine Love and Wisdom   42

53

[P]hysical sight could not occur without an organ of sight, the eye; nor can inner sight, or thought, occur without an organized substance as its source. . . .

Arcana Coelestia   444

[L]ove constitutes the whole person; the nature of any individual is determined by the nature of that individual's love.

Arcana Coelestia   10177:4

People know that love exists, but they do not know what love is. . . . They are quite unaware that it is our very life—not just the general life of the whole body and the general life of all our thoughts but also the life of all their details. A perceptive person can grasp this when someone says, "If you take away the affection that comes from love, can you think anything? Can you do anything? As the influence of love cools, doesn't thought cool, and speech and action?"

Divine Love and Wisdom   1

There are many derivatives of love that have been assigned names like affections, desires, appetites, and their pleasures and joys; and there are many derivatives of wisdom, like perception, reflection, memory, thought, and attention to a subject. There are still more derivatives of love and wisdom both, such as agreement, decision, and choice to act, among others. Actually, all these derivatives stem from both love and wisdom, but we assign them to the source that is stronger and closer to hand.

Divine Love and Wisdom   363

No one's life love can occur without derivatives, which are called affections. The affections of a hellish love, properly called cravings, are specific evils; and the affections of heavenly love, properly called delights, are specific good things. A love dwells in its affections like a lord in his dominion or a king in his kingdom. Their dominion or regency is over the elements of the mind, that is, the elements of a person's intentionality and discernment, and thereby over the body. A person's life

love, through its affections and consequent perceptions and
through its pleasures and consequent thoughts, governs the
whole person.

Divine Providence   106:2

We have two abilities that constitute our life; one is called
intentionality, and the other is called discernment. These are
distinguishable from each other, but they have been so created as to be one; and when they are one, they are called the
mind. . . .

As everything in the universe that is in accord with the divine design goes back to the good and the true, so everything
in a person goes back to intentionality and discernment, since
the good in a person is a matter of intentionality and the true
in a person is a matter of discernment. In fact, these two abilities, or these two lives of an individual, are their recipients and
subjects. Intentionality is the recipient and subject of all elements of the good, and discernment is the recipient and subject of all elements of the true. And since the good and the
true in a person are here and nowhere else, so too are love and
faith since love is a matter of the good and the good, a matter
of love, while faith is a matter of the true and the true, a matter of faith.

The New Jerusalem and Its Heavenly Doctrine   29.

There is a general recognition that we have an ability to discern (which is called rationality) and an ability to think, intend, say, and do what we discern, which is a freedom. . . . But
we need to realize first that all freedom is a matter of love, to
the point that love and freedom are one thing. Everything we
have that brings us joy comes from our love, . . . [and our] joy
leads us along the way a river carries things along with its current. . . .

Divine Providence   73:2

*Throughout the course of his providence, the Lord keeps these
two abilities* [rationality and freedom] *safe and guards them as
holy.* This is because without these two abilities, we would not

have discernment and intentionality and, therefore, would not
be human. It is also because, without them, we could not be
united to the Lord and, therefore, could not be reformed and
reborn; and because, without these two abilities, we would
not have immortality and eternal life.

Divine Providence 96

It has not been common knowledge until now that there
are three vertical levels in every individual. This is because
these levels have not been identified; and as long as these levels remain obscure, only continuous levels can be recognized.
And when only these levels are recognized, people can believe
that love and wisdom increase in a person only along a continuum. But it needs to be realized that there are in every individual from birth three vertical or distinct levels and that each
vertical or distinct level also has horizontal or continuous levels by which there can be an increase along a continuum. . . .

We call these three vertical levels natural, spiritual, and
heavenly. . . . When we are born, we first arrive on the natural
level, and this increases in us along a continuum according to
our factual learning and the discernment we gain through it,
all the way to that peak of discernment we call rationality.
However, the second level, called the spiritual, is not opened
by this achievement but by a love of uses derived from discernment or by a spiritual love of uses, which love is a love toward the neighbor. This level, likewise, can increase along a
continuum to its peak, and it increases through insights into
what is true and good, or through spiritual truths. Still, the
third level, called the heavenly, is not opened by these but is
opened by a heavenly love of uses, which love is a love for the
Lord. Love for the Lord is simply committing the precepts of
the Word to life, which, in essence, is avoiding evils because
they are hellish and demonic and doing what is good because
it is heavenly and divine.

Divine Love and Wisdom 236–237

Since three levels of love and wisdom—and, therefore, of
use—occur in us, it follows that there occur in us three levels

of intentionality and discernment; and, therefore, of decision; and, therefore, of focus into use. Intentionality is the recipient of love, and discernment is the recipient of wisdom; and decision is a matter of the use that results from them. We can see from this that there is in every individual a natural, a spiritual, and a heavenly intentionality and discernment—potentially from birth and actually when they are opened. In a word, the human mind, consisting of intentionality and discernment, consists of three levels from creation and from birth, so everyone has a natural mind, a spiritual mind and a heavenly mind; and we can for this reason be raised up into angelic wisdom and possess it while we are living in this world. Still, we do not enter into it until after death, if we become angels; and then we say unutterable things, things the natural person cannot understand.

Divine Love and Wisdom 239

There are two things that emanate from the Lord, which are the source of everything in the heavens and in the earths, namely the Divine-True and the Divine-Good. The Divine-True is the source of all intelligence and wisdom in angels and mortals, and the Divine-Good is the source of all compassion and love in them. These two emanate from the Lord united; so in their very origin they are one. But in the angels and mortals who receive them, they are two because there are two recipient vessels of life in them, called discernment and intentionality. Discernment is the recipient of the Divine-True, and intentionality is the recipient of the Divine-Good. . . . [T]o the extent that these two, the Divine-True and the Divine-Good, are one in angels or mortals, the angels or mortals are united with the Lord; but to the extent that they are not one, they are not thus united.

The Apocalypse Explained 466

The central characteristic of love is not loving oneself but loving others and being united to them through love. The central characteristic of love is being loved by others and so being, in fact, united. The essence of all love consists of

57

union—this is, in fact, its life, which is called joy, charm, de-light, sweetness, blessedness, contentment, and happiness. Love consists in having one's own belong to another and in feeling another's joy as joy in oneself: that is loving. But feeling one's own joy in another and not the other's in oneself is not loving; this is loving oneself; the other is loving the neighbor.

Divine Love and Wisdom 47

All evils and their consequent falsities, both hereditary and ac-quired, live in the natural mind. [This] . . . is because that mind is a [natural] world in form or image, while the spiritual mind is a heaven in form or image, and evil cannot be made welcome in heaven. So from birth, this latter mind is not opened but has only the potentiality of being opened.

Divine Love and Wisdom 270

The Universal Human

The only form in which any angel in heaven can perceive the divine is the human form; and, remarkable as it may seem, in the higher heavens, they cannot even think about the divine in any other way. This necessity is borne in upon them by the di-vine itself as it flows in and also by the form of heaven, which governs the way their own thoughts reach out around them.

Heaven and Hell 79

It is a mystery still unknown in this world that heaven in its entirety resolves into a single person, but this is common knowledge in the heavens. Knowing this and its specific and individual corollaries is the heart of angelic intelligence there. Many things depend on this, which, without it as their general principle, would not enter crisply and clearly into the concepts of their minds. Because they know that all the heavens and all their communities resolve into a single person, they call heaven the *Universal and Divine Human*—divine because the Lord's Divine makes heaven.

Heaven and Hell 59

All things true, like all things good . . . are arranged in heaven in such a design that one focuses on another in a form like that of the human body, whose members, organs, and viscera (or their uses) . . . focus on each other and so work that they are one. This [the design things true and good are in] is why heaven is called the Universal Human. Its very life is from the Lord, who from himself arranges everything in this design. So heaven is an image and likeness of the Lord. When things true are arranged in the design heaven is in, they are in a heavenly design and are capable of entering the good. The true and good things in every angel are in this kind of design, and the true and good things in every mortal who is being regenerated are being arranged in this design.

Arcana Coelestia 4302:3

Even though everything of a person's body does correspond to everything of heaven, still, a person is not an image of heaven in outward form but in inward form. It is our more inward reaches that accept heaven, while our more outward reaches accept the world. So, to the extent that our more inward reaches do accept heaven, we are heavens in least form, after the image of the universal. But to the extent that our more inward reaches are not receptive, we are not heavens and images of the universal. Still, our more outward aspects, which are receptive of the world, can be in a form suited to the design of this world and, therefore, more or less beautiful. Outward beauty, physical beauty, comes from our parents and from our formation in the womb and is thereafter maintained by a general inflow from this world. This is why the form of the natural person may be radically different from the form of his or her spiritual person.

Heaven and Hell 99

The design is that heavenly things should govern spiritual ones; through them should govern natural things; and, finally, through these latter, should govern physical things. But when physical and natural things domineer over spiritual and heavenly things, the design has been demolished; and when the

59

design has been demolished, there is an image of hell. So the design is restored by the Lord through regeneration; and when it has been restored, then there is an image of heaven. This is how people are rescued from hell by the Lord, and this is how they are raised into heaven.

To show, then, how the correspondence of the outer person to the inner person works, I may explain briefly. Every regenerated person is a kind of tiny heaven, or a likeness or image of the whole heaven; so, in the Word, the inner person is called "heaven." In heaven, the design is such that the Lord governs spiritual matters through heavenly ones and natural matters through spiritual ones, and thus governs the whole heaven as a single person; so heaven is called the universal human. This kind of order also exists in every individual who is in heaven. When someone is like this, then he or she is likewise a tiny heaven, or (which is the same thing) a kingdom of the Lord, because the kingdom of the Lord is within him or her. For such an individual, outward things correspond to inward ones the way they do in heaven—that is, they are obedient.

Arcana Coelestia 911

CHAPTER 5

The Human Process

·

The previous chapter focused on freedom and rationality, love and wisdom, as constants of our human nature, leaving us with a relatively static picture. Without such constants, we are hard pressed to find coherence in the varied flow of experience, but we know very well indeed that we are not static. It often seems that the most constant thing about our lives is change, and unpredictable change at that. Circumstances change, and we ourselves change. Swedenborg was deeply concerned to call us to be purposeful about the changes in ourselves and calls us to attend to the direction in which we are moving spiritually.

Any picture of our human condition would be romantic indeed if it did not take into full account the obvious wrongs that plague as individuals and as societies. Swedenborg takes sharp issue with the doctrine of "original sin" if that is taken to mean that we are born guilty and, therefore, are damned. He insists, however, that we are born *inclined* to "evil." In terms of the preceding chapter, we are born "in inverted order," more sensitive to our lower loves than to our higher ones. We are more sensitive to our own pleasures and pains than to those of others and, therefore, tend spontaneously to protect our own interests at the expense of others. It is the central task of our earthly lives to do our part in reversing this hierarchy.

Significantly, Swedenborg's most complete outline of the lifelong process of "regeneration" or rebirth is found among the very first paragraphs of his first published theological work, *Arcana Coelestia*. It rests on the symbolic base of the seven days of creation in the first chapters of Genesis. Briefly, the process is initiated and fueled by the Lord's mercy. Our part involves learning that there is a higher way and striving to follow that way. This is what enables the Divine to reorder our loves.

It is not an easy path to follow, primarily because it means going against what feels most natural to us and abandoning the "certainties" that give us a sense of security. However, fidelity to the ideal leads to fundamental change; and, ultimately, inner conflict is succeeded by an inner peace and wholeness that are the only solid foundations of heavenly community.

Here we begin to approach another of Swedenborg's more radical assertions, namely, that in the person of Jesus Christ, the Divine so clothed itself in our nature that it went through, on an infinite scale, the same process that is required of us. At the center of his system, then, is an intensely personal doctrine of transformation, of process, rather than a static doctrine of abstract, unchanging structure.

Where We Start

Brute animals act only through the loves and derived affections into which they were created and have since been born. In fact, each animal is borne wherever its affection and love takes it. Because of this, they have access to all the information that is proper to their love. They actually know, from a love that imitates marriage love, how to mate—cattle in one way, birds in another. Birds know how to make nests, how to lay their eggs and brood over them, how to hatch their chicks and feed them, all without any instruction, just from the love like marriage love and from a love of offspring, which have all this information built into them. . . .

If human beings were in the design into which they were created—that is, in love toward the neighbor and in love to the Lord, since these loves are properly human—then, more than all animals, they would be born with not only information but also with all spiritual truths and heavenly goodness and, therefore, with all wisdom and intelligence. . . . But since they are born not into the design but contrary to it, they are born into ignorance of everything; and because of this, things are so arranged that they can then be reborn and thereby come into as much intelligence and wisdom as they do goodness. . . .

Arcana Coelestia 6323:2–3

We have been so created that everything we intend and think and do seems to us to be in ourselves and, therefore, from ourselves. Without this appearance, we would not be human since we could not accept, hold, or seem to possess anything of the good and the true, or of love and wisdom, because, without this seemingly lifelike appearance, we could have no union with God and, therefore, no eternal life. But if we use this appearance to adopt a belief that we do intend and think and do what is good on our own and not from the Lord (though in all appearance it is on our own), then we turn the good into evil within ourselves and make the origin of evil within ourselves. . . .

Only God is good, and there is nothing intrinsically good except from God. So, anyone who focuses on God and wants to be led by God is involved in the good; and anyone who turns away from God and wants to be led by self is not involved in the good. For the good that such an individual does is either for the sake of self or for worldly ends, so it is either for credit or simply imitative or hypocritical. We can see from this that humanity itself is the source of evil—not that this source was inherent in humanity from creation but that human beings adopted it by turning away from God toward themselves.

Marital Love 444

The origin of evil is from the abuse of the abilities of rationality and freedom.

Divine Love and Wisdom 264

We are all born into an involvement in self-love and love of the world from our parents. All the evil that by constant practice has become, as it were, second nature is passed on to one's offspring, which has occurred cumulatively in a long sequence from parents, grandparents, and great-grandparents. So the derived accumulation of evil has become so great that the whole life of our self-image is entirely evil. This chain is broken and changed only by a life of faith and compassion from the Lord.

Arcana Coelestia 8550

As soon as we are born, we are brought into a state of innocence, so that this can be a plane for other states and a core within them. . . . Then, we are brought into a state of good, heavenly affection, which is the state of love for parents and which for [infants] takes the place of love for the Lord. . . .

Arcana Coelestia 3183

The human self-image [*proprium*] . . . is nothing but evil and, when it is presented to view, is terribly misshapen. But when compassion and innocence are instilled into the self-image by the Lord, then it looks good and attractive. . . . Compassion and innocence are what not only excuse but virtually wipe out what is evil and false in us, as we can see in infants. When they are loving each other and their parents, and their infant innocence is shining through, then even actual evil and false characteristics are not just unnoticeable but even pleasing.

Arcana Coelestia 164

Outlines of the Process

When we are being reborn, we are then kept in a kind of intermediate good by the Lord: this good serves to pave the way for things genuinely good and true. But after these good and true things have been brought in, we are separated from that [intermediate good]. Anyone who is at all knowledgeable about rebirth and the new person can grasp the fact that the new person is quite different from the old one. The new person is involved in an affection for spiritual and heavenly things, . . . while the old person is in affections for worldly and earthly things. . . .

When someone is becoming a new person . . . , that is, being reborn, it does not happen instantly, as some people believe, but over many years—in fact, through our whole life, right up to the last. . . .

It is recognized that we have one state in infancy, another in childhood, another in adolescence, another in maturity, and another in old age. It is also recognized that we shed our state of infancy and its games when we make the passage into the state of childhood and that we shed the state of childhood when we make the passage into the state of adolescence; shed this, in turn, when we make the passage into the state of maturity; and shed this again when we make the passage into the state of old age. And if we reflect, we can also recognize that each age has its delights and that, through these, in sequence, we are led to those appropriate to the next age—that these delights serve to bring us through from one stage to another, eventually to the delight in intelligence and wisdom appropriate to old age.

Arcana Coelestia 4063:2–4

Everyone is born with bodily awareness and then comes into sensory awareness, awareness of the natural world, and eventually rational awareness; and, if the process does not stall there, he becomes spiritually aware. The reason for this progression is that [the earlier stages] form planes that higher stages rest on, the way a palace rests on its foundations.

Marital Love 447

It is, in fact, recognized that we are born with no information and without any rational ability but only with the ability to receive them. Thereafter, step by step, we learn and absorb everything, primarily through sense impressions of hearing and sight; and as we learn and absorb things, we become rational. We can see that this happens by way of the body—that is, by an external way—because it happens through hearing and sight. But what we do not recognize is that all the while something is flowing in from within that accepts the things that are entering and slipping in from the outside and arranges them in a pattern. What is flowing in and accepting and arranging is good, heavenly, and divine, because it comes from the Lord. . . .

Arcana Coelestia 2557

It is recognized that we get evil from both our parents and that this evil is called inherited evil. We are born involved in it, but it does not become obvious except as we grow older and act from discernment and intentionality. In the meantime, it lies hidden, especially in infancy. . . . Even though [infants] seem to be in a state of innocence, still this inherited evil is latent in everything they do. . . . But when we are reborn, the Lord brings us through into a state of new infancy and eventually into heavenly wisdom and, therefore, into true infancy or innocence; for true infancy or innocence dwells in wisdom.

Arcana Coelestia 4563:2

This [biblical passage, Genesis 29:33] deals . . . with the progression of human rebirth from the outer to the inner, that is, from the truth of faith to the good of compassion. The truth that belongs to faith is outward and the good that belongs to compassion is inward. If the truth that belongs to faith is to be alive, it must be brought into our intentionality in order to receive life there. The true does not, in fact, live by knowing but by intending: through a new intending that the Lord creates within us, life flows in from him. The first life shows itself in obedience, which is the first form of intentionality; the second shows itself through an affection for doing what is true, which is an advanced intentionality that exists when delight and blessedness are felt in doing what is true. Unless the progression of faith is of this kind, the true does not become true but becomes something divorced from life.

Arcana Coelestia 3870

When we are being regenerated by the Lord, it is like this: at first, we are involved in what is true but not in any goodness of life because of what is true. Next, we are involved in goodness of life as a result of what is true but not yet as a result of what is good. Finally, when we have been reborn, we are involved in goodness of life because of what is good; and then we become aware of the true and multiply it in ourselves because of what is good.

Arcana Coelestia   6396

The Lord is present with everyone, urging and pressing to be accepted. And when we accept him (which happens when we recognize him as God the Creator, Redeemer, and Regenerator), this is his first coming, which is called the dawn. From this time on, we begin to be mentally enlightened concerning spiritual matters and to move into ever deeper and deeper wisdom. As we accept this wisdom from the Lord, we come [from dawn] through morning into daytime, a daytime that lasts through our old age all the way to our death. After this, we come to the Lord himself in heaven, where, even though we may have died in old age, we return to the morning of our life; and the beginnings of wisdom that have taken root in the natural world grow to eternity.

True Christian Religion   766

Wisdom and love emanate from the Lord as a sun and flow into heaven, generally and specifically, which is where angels get their wisdom and love. They also flow generally and specifically into this world, which is where we get our wisdom and love. But while they emanate from the Lord united and flow into the souls of angels and mortals united, they are not received united into our [conscious] minds. Light is accepted first there, which forms discernment; and love, which forms intentionality, is accepted gradually. This too is from providence because we all need to be created anew (that is, reformed), and this is accomplished by means of our discernment. Actually, we must from infancy absorb insights into what is true and good, which teach us to live well, that is, to

67

intend and act rightly. So, our intentionality is formed by means of our discernment. This is why we have been given the ability to raise our discernment almost into the light heaven's angels are in—so that we may see what we should intend and, therefore, do in order to be temporarily prosperous here in the world, and blessed to eternity after death.

Intercourse between the Soul and the Body 14

The Six Days

[Swedenborg takes the six days of creation as symbolic of six successive stages of spiritual growth. The following is his summary, which introduces a verse-by-verse, full-chapter treatment. *Editor*]

The six days or times, which are six successive states of human rebirth, are in general terms like this.

The *first* state is the one that precedes—both the state from infancy and the state just before rebirth. It is called void, emptiness, and darkness. And the first motion, which is the Lord's mercy, is the spirit of God hovering over the face of the water.

The *second* state is one in which a distinction is made between the things that are the Lord's and the things that belong to the person. The things that are the Lord's are called "the remnants" in the Word and are primarily insights of faith that have been learned from infancy. These are stored away and do not surface until the person reaches this state, which rarely happens nowadays without trial, misfortune, or depression, which deaden the physical and worldly concerns that are typically human. In this way, the concerns of the outer person are separated from those of the inner. The remnants are in the inner person, stored away there by the Lord for this time and for this use.

The *third* state is one of repentance, in which the individual, from the inner person, does talk reverently and devoutly and does bring forth good [actions] that resemble deeds of compassion. Still, they are not really alive because they are thought

68

to be done independently. They're called the tender plant, the seed-bearing plant, and, finally, the fruit tree.

The *fourth* state occurs when the individual is moved by love and enlightened by faith. Before this, the person did indeed talk reverently and bring forth good [actions]—but out of a state of trial and constraint, not out of faith and compassion. So now faith and compassion are kindled in the inner person and are called the two great lights.

The *fifth* state is the one in which the individual talks from faith and, consequently, strengthens his or her devotion to what is true and good. The things now brought forth are alive and are called the fish of the sea and the birds of the air.

The *sixth* state occurs when the person says what is true and does what is good from faith and, therefore, from love. The things now brought forth are called the living soul and the animals. And since the individual is then beginning to act from both faith and love, he or she becomes a spiritual person, who is called an image [of God]. The spiritual life of such a person is delighted and nourished by things related to insights of faith and to deeds of compassion, which are called "food"; and the natural life is delighted and nourished by things related to the body and the senses. This results in conflicts until love gains control, and the person becomes heavenly.

Not all people who are being reborn reach this state. Some—most people nowadays—reach only the first; some, only the second. Some reach the third, fourth, and fifth; few, the sixth; and hardly anyone, the seventh.

Arcana Coelestia   6–13

The Struggle

Before anything is brought back into order, it is quite normal for it to be brought first into a kind of confusion, a virtual chaos. It this way, things that fit together badly are severed from each other; and when they have been severed, then the Lord arranges them in order.

Arcana Coelestia   842:3

We have been dealing with the state of loneliness people are in when they are being re-formed and becoming spiritual. Now we deal with their restoration, with comfort and their hope of help. People nowadays are unaware that, when they are being re-formed, they are brought into ignorance of what is true or loneliness, even into pain and hopelessness; and that only then do they receive comfort and help from the Lord. The reason for this ignorance is that not many people are being re-formed.

The primary purpose of this depression and loneliness is that the second-hand faith [*persuasivum*] they have tried to maintain for their self-image may be broken . . . and that they may accept some perception of what is good and true. They cannot accept this until the second-hand faith derived from their self-image has been softened, so to speak. A state of anxiety and pain that reaches all the way to hopelessness accomplishes this. No one can grasp with full sensitivity what is good, what is blessed and happy, without having been in a state of not-good, not-blessed, and not-happy.

Arcana Coelestia 2694:2

The issue in our [deeper] trials is whether the evil will gain control that is in us from hell or the good that is in us from the Lord. The evil that wants control is in the natural or outer person, while the good is in the spiritual or inner person. As a result, even in our trials, the issue is the control of one over the other. If the evil wins, then the natural person controls the spiritual; if the good wins, then the spiritual person controls the natural.

Arcana Coelestia 8961

People in the midst of trials are likely to drop their hands and give themselves over entirely to prayers, which they pour out passionately, not realizing that prayers [by themselves] do not work and that they have to fight against the false and evil things that the hells are injecting. . . .

Arcana Coelestia 8179

([W]hen we are being reborn) our first state is a tranquil one; but as we are making the passage into the new life, we pass also into a state of disturbance. The evil and false things we have absorbed in the past are coming out . . . and disturbing us, eventually with such force that we are caught in trials and harassments by the hellish crew, which is trying to destroy the state of our new life. Still, at the deepest level, we have a state of peace. Unless this were at our deepest level, we would not fight. We are actually focusing on it as our goal throughout the struggles we are involved in, and unless it were our goal, we would not have the energy or the strength to fight.

Arcana Coelestia 3696:2

There were some people who, in this world, had believed in instantaneous salvation by direct grace; and when they had become spirits, they wanted their hellish delight, their delight in what is evil, to be transformed by divine omnipotence and divine grace into heavenly delight and delight in what is good. Since they longed for this, it was allowed that some angels should do it, so they then removed their hellish delight. But since this was the delight of their life's love, actually their very life, they lay there as though they were dead, without sensation or motion; and it was impossible to breathe into them any life but their own.

Divine Providence 338:7

In order that we may be capable of self-examination, we have been given the capacity to discern, and that capacity has been separated from our intentionality so that we can know and discern and admit what is good and what is evil. We can see, that is, what the quality of our intentions is, what we love, and what we crave. . . . When we see ourselves in this mirror, so to speak, and recognize what is sinful, then, if we ask the Lord's help, we can stop intending it, avoid it, and then work against it, if not freely then at least by force of [inner] struggle, eventually coming to dislike and even detest it.

Divine Providence 278

71

The Goal

Divine peace arises from the union of the Lord with heaven and, in particular, in each angel from the union of the good and the true; so when angels are in a state of love, they are in a state of peace because then the good is united to the true within them. . . . It is like this for people who are being regenerated. When a union of the good and the true occurs within them, which happens especially after temptation-trials, then they come into a state of delight that derives from heavenly peace.

This [heavenly] peace is like the morn or dawn in spring—the night is past, all earthly things are filled anew with life at the rising of the sun; the scent of plants is wafted here and there by downdrift of the dew. The gentle breath of springtime gives the soul fertility and fills our minds with charm; and this because the morn or dawn in springtime answers to the state of peace that angels have in heaven.

Heaven and Hell 289

No one can know what the restful peace of the outer person is like, or the restlessness brought on by cravings and falsities, who has not experienced a state of peace. This state is so full of delight that it overflows every concept of delight. It is not just the ending of struggle but is a life that comes from a more inward peace, moving the outer person in ways beyond description. Then truths of faith and good gifts of love are born that draw their life from the delight of peace.

Arcana Coelestia 92

The Model

We can see in our regeneration, as in a kind of image, how the Lord glorified his human [nature] or (which is the same thing) made it divine. In fact, just as the Lord wholly changed his human state into a divine one, so . . . when he is regenerating us, he wholly changes our state and makes a new person out of the old one.

Arcana Coelestia 3296:2

When the Lord made his human [nature] divine, he followed the same pattern that he follows when he is making us new by regeneration; namely, from outward matters to more inward ones and, therefore, from the true that is in the lowest part of the design to the good that is more inward and is called spiritual good, and, from there, to heavenly good.

Arcana Coelestia 4585:2

The Lord followed the whole divine design from earliest infancy, to heavenly things and in heavenly things. . . . Everyone who is being created anew by the Lord is brought along in a design like this, but the design varies according to individual nature and character.

Arcana Coelestia 1554

CHAPTER 6

The Good Life

.

The views of human structure and human process sketched in the previous two chapters presuppose ethical principles. If our freedom is to have any meaning, there must be values that guide our choices. If the goal of this life is regeneration in the context of community, there is need of some notion of the discipline appropriate to that change.

Swedenborgians have shied away from labelling Emanuel Swedenborg as a "mystic," largely, one suspects, because he does not hold out enlightenment or altered states of consciousness as goals and does not advocate any meditative or "spiritual" discipline. For him, the life we are designed for is a very down-to-earth life of thoughtful and productive participation in human society. His own spirituality was grounded in such a life, as witnessed by his active participation in Sweden's political life well into his old age. About a year before his death, for example, he substantially enlarged a treatise on monetary policy that he had published almost fifty years earlier and published the new version in an effort to counter what he saw as short-sighted devices for dealing with unfavorable exchange rates. Heaven, for him, was a realm of active service rather than of passive contemplation; and an adequate foundation for heaven was, therefore, to be found in active service here and now.

Yet he was no advocate of activity for activity's sake or for some kind of scorecard system that balanced good deeds against bad ones. The quality of motivation is absolutely critical. Service done for self-serving reasons simply confirms

74

the individual's egotism and disrespect for others. Service done for truly religious reasons transforms the individual who performs it, constituting the solid foundation of a heavenly character. To take credit for one's good deeds is to cross from righteousness into self-righteousness. Instead, we are to use our apparent independence thoughtfully, choosing deeds of compassion; and are, on reflection, to acknowledge that the ability to do so is a gift from our Lord and not our possession.

Compassion is to be exercised with discrimination. In keeping with his principle of the inseparability of love and wisdom, Swedenborg insists that we are to use our intelligence to look as honestly as we can at the actual effects of our actions. Simply doing what other people want us to do, giving to all who ask, may do more harm than good. He would instantly have recognized and endorsed the idea of "tough love," the kind of love that is not ruled by a need for approval.

Formal worship and, we may suppose, church membership (which was not an issue when it was virtually universal) may play a constructive role in this, but not as ends in themselves. Consistent with his practical bent, Swedenborg sees them as useful only to the extent that they guide and support the living of constructive lives in "secular" society. The essential rules for such constructive living, rules analogous to the Ten Commandments, are to be found in every religion. When they are followed (again "for religious reasons"), they work. In other words, every religion in its own distinctive way teaches the path to heaven.

General Considerations

Some people believe that it is hard to live the life that leads to heaven, which is called a spiritual life, because they have heard that you have to renounce the world and give up the desires people associate with the body and the flesh and "live spiritually." All they understand by this is rejecting worldly concerns (especially concerns with money and prestige) and going around in constant devout meditation about God, salvation, and eternal life, spending one's life in prayer and in reading the Word and devotional books. . . . But people who renounce the world and "live by the spirit" in this way acquire a mournful life, one that is not receptive of heavenly joy. . . . Rather, in order to be receptive of heaven's life, we should by all means live in the world and be involved in its duties and business. In this way, through a moral and civic life, we accept a spiritual life. There is no other way spiritual life can take shape in us, no other way our spirits can be prepared for heaven.

Heaven and Hell 528

It is (the purpose) of divine providence that people should act from freedom according to reason.

Divine Providence 71

First place in the doctrine of compassion is taken by this principle—that the beginning of compassion is not to do evil to the neighbor and the second, to do the neighbor good.

True Christian Religion 435

It should also be known that, in deeds or works, the whole person is presented and that our intentionality and thought (which are our more inward things) are not complete until they exist in deeds or works (which are our more outward things). Deeds and works are actually the outmost things in which those [inward] aspects find their boundaries; without boundaries, they are undefined, so to speak, like things that have not yet emerged and are, therefore, not yet part of us.

Heaven and Hell 475

Our deeds are only gestures and, seen apart from intentionality, are only motions variously shaped and coordinated—rather like the movements of a machine—and, therefore, soulless. But deeds seen together with their intentionality are not motions like this. Instead, they are forms of intentionality presented to the eye, since deeds are nothing but witnesses to the kinds of things that are happening in the intentionality. They even have their soul or life from their intentionality. So we can say of deeds much the same thing that we say of motions— that in deeds nothing is living but intentionality, as in motions nothing is living but energy [*conatus*]. People recognize this because intelligent folk do not pay attention to deeds but simply to the intent from which, through which, and for which the deeds occur. In fact, a wise person scarcely sees the deeds but sees the quality and intensity of the intent within them.

Arcana Coelestia 9293

But by deeds and works we do not mean deeds and works simply as they appear in outward form. Everyone is aware that every deed and work issue from our intentionality and thought. Unless they did issue from that source, they would be nothing but motions, like those of machines and robots. . . .

A thousand people can do the same thing, that is, can present deeds that look alike. These deeds can be so much alike that one can scarcely detect any difference in their outward form. And yet each one, seen in its own right, is different because it comes from a different intent.

For example, take acting candidly and honestly toward a friend. One person may do so with a view to seeming candid and honest for the sake of self and prestige; another, for the sake of the world and for money; a third, for reward and credit; a fourth, to curry friendship; a fifth, out of fear of the law, of losing reputation and position; a sixth, to inveigle someone into partisanship for evil ends; a seventh, to deceive; and others, for other purposes. Even though all their deeds seem good (since acting candidly and honestly toward a friend is good), they are still evil because they are not being done for the sake of candor and honesty but for the sake of self and the world, which are the objects of their love. Candor and honesty are servants of this love, like household servants whose master belittles and dismisses them when they do not serve him.

Heaven and Hell 472

We should first state who the neighbor is, since it is the neighbor who is to be loved and toward whom our care is to be extended. . . . [T]he neighbor is not just the individual person but also people in the collective sense. It is the community, smaller or larger; it is the nation; it is the church; it is the Lord's kingdom; and, above all, it is the Lord. These are increasing levels of the neighbor.

The New Jerusalem and Its Heavenly Doctrine 84; 91

When people are in ignorance, all they can know is that any good they do is their own and anything true they think is their own. It is the same as for people who lay claim to any good things they do and take credit for them, unaware then that these things are not good, even though they seem to be, and unaware that the self-image and credit they are investing in their deeds are evil and false things that darken and becloud. . . . The quality and amount of the evil and false within them lie hidden so that this can never be seen in physical life as it can in the other life. [Inner] things are then open to view completely, as though in broad daylight. But it is different if this happens out of ignorance and is not absolutized; then these evil and false things are easily dispelled. But if people confirm themselves in the notion that they can do what is good and resist what is evil from their own proper strength, then this remains attached to them and makes the good evil and the true false. Still, the design is such that we ought to do what is good as though we were independent and, therefore, should not drop our hands and think "If I can't do anything good on my own, then I'd better wait for some direct inflow," and stand there passively: this too is contrary to the design. No, we ought to do what is good as though we were independent; but when we reflect on the good we are doing or have done, then we should think, recognize, and believe that the Lord has been doing this through us.

Arcana Coelestia 1712:1–2

Having dealt with faith, compassion, and freedom of choice, we come next in sequence to repentance because true faith and genuine compassion are impossible without repentance and no one can perform repentance without freedom of choice. Another reason for dealing with repentance at this point is that no one can be reborn until the more serious evils . . . have been put aside, and they are put aside by means of repentance.

True Christian Religion 509

You may ask how we are to perform repentance. The answer is that we should do it genuinely, which means exploring ourselves, recognizing and acknowledging our sins, asking the Lord's help, and beginning a new life. We have shown in the preceding section that there can be no repentance without exploration. But what is the point of exploring except to recognize our sins? And what is the point of recognizing them unless we admit that they are within us? And what is the point of these three steps unless we confess our sins before the Lord; ask for help; and, with that help, begin a new life, since a new life is the whole point? This is genuine repentance.

True Christian Religion 530

Laws of Life

Where there is no compassion, selfishness is present and particularly a hatred for everyone who does not agree. This is why such people see nothing in their neighbors except what is wrong with them; and if they see anything good, they either regard it as insignificant or find a bad interpretation for it. . . . But compassionate people scarcely see what is wrong with others. Instead, they are alert to everything in them that is good and true, even putting a good interpretation on things that are evil and false. All angels are like this and receive this attitude from the Lord, who bends everything toward the good.

Arcana Coelestia 1079

The inner aspect of compassion and mercy is to look carefully at just who it is that one ought to help and what their

79

quality is and how to help each one. People who have finally been brought through to the inner aspect of compassion and mercy know that the essential internal is to will well and to help the inner person, using, therefore, those things that nurture spiritual life. They know that the outer aspect is to help the outer person, using, therefore, things that nurture physical life. But this latter needs always to be done with care that, while we help the outer person, we help the inner at the same time. For if we help the outer and harm the inner, we are not exercising compassion; so while we are doing the one, we need to focus on the other.

Arcana Coelestia 9209:2

The evils listed in the Ten Commandments contain within them all the evils that can ever occur. . . .

Apocalypse Explained 935:2

All the nations . . . that have any religion have laws like those in the Ten Commandments; and everyone who lives by them for religious reasons is saved, and everyone who does not live by them for religious reasons is damned.

Apocalypse Revealed 529:2

The first three commandments have to do with love to the Lord; the last six, with love toward the neighbor; and the fourth commandment, which is "Honor your father and mother," is an intermediate commandment. . . .

Apocalypse Explained 1026:3

But since union cannot be achieved unless there is some reciprocity, . . . the Lord has endowed us with the freedom of intending and acting in apparent independence. . . . So while we are uniting ourselves with the Lord by means of the last six commandments, apparently with our own strength, the Lord is uniting himself to us by means of the first three. . . . We have no belief in these [first three commandments] unless we refrain from the sins implied in the last six commandments.

Apocalypse Explained 1027:3–4

For people on earth, heaven is to recognize the Divine and to be led by the Divine. The first and foremost principle of every religion is the recognition of the Divine, and the rules of every religion center in worship—in how the Divine is to be revered in order to be accepted. . . . A moral life may be lived for the sake of the Divine or for the sake of people in this world. These two look alike outwardly, but they are inwardly quite different. For the person who is living a moral life for the sake of the Divine is being led by the Divine, but the one who is living a moral life for the sake of people in this world is self-led.

Heaven and Hell 319

[T]rue worship consists of fulfilling uses and, therefore, expressing compassion in action. If people believe that serving the Lord consists only of regular church attendance, listening to sermons, and praying, that these are adequate, they are sadly mistaken. Real worship of the Lord consists of fulfilling uses; and uses, while we are living in this world, are for each of us properly to fulfill his or her function in his or her position. This means putting our hearts into service to our country, our community, and our neighbor; it means acting with candor toward our associates and performing our duties with care according to our several abilities. These uses are the primary forms of the exercise of compassion and the primary means of worshipping the Lord. Church attendance, listening to sermons, and prayer are also necessary, but they are worthless apart from these uses since they are not [substantive matters] of life but teach what life ought to be like.

Arcana Coelestia 7038

Fame and wealth may be blessings or curses. Everyday experience witnesses that both devout and impious people, both honest and dishonest people—both good and evil people, that is—gain fame and wealth. . . .

Anyone can learn why fame and wealth may be blessings and why they may be curses by just thinking rationally about it. They are blessings for people who do not set their hearts on them. Setting one's heart on them is loving oneself in them, and not setting one's heart on them is loving the usefulness they bring, rather than oneself. . . . We may add that fame and wealth seduce some people and do not seduce others. They are seductive when they arouse the loves associated with our self-image, . . . and they are not seductive when they do not arouse that love.

Divine Providence 217:1–2

We all need to take care that we have the necessities of life—food, clothing, shelter, and the other things that are held necessary in the civic life we are involved in. This holds true not just for ourselves but also for those who depend on us, and not just for the present but for the future as well. For unless we do acquire the necessities of life, we cannot be in a state to exercise compassion, being actually in need of everything ourselves.

The New Jerusalem and Its Heavenly Doctrine 97

Earlier, I have been allowed to mention that people may acquire wealth and accumulate as much of a fortune as may be, provided they do not do this deviously and by exploitation [*arte mala*]. They may eat well and drink, provided they do not make this the chief goal of their lives; their houses may be as impressive as their circumstances allow; they may carry on conversations like anyone else, go to the theater, discuss worldly affairs—there is no need to go around looking pious, sad, and grieving, with their heads drooping. They can be happy and cheerful. There is no need to give their possessions to the poor except as affection leads them to. In a word, they can live in outward form just like worldly people. All this is no hindrance to their entry into heaven, provided they are inwardly suitably mindful of God and deal candidly and equitably with the neighbor.

Heaven and Hell 358

A rich person can in many ways be more help [to country and neighbor] than a poor one . . . .

Heaven and Hell 361:2

Many people believe that love toward the neighbor means giving to the poor, helping the needy, and doing good to everybody. But compassion means acting with care that the results will be good. If we help a poor or needy evildoer, we do evil to the neighbor through that evildoer because we reinforce the person in the evil by the help we give and supply the means of doing harm to others.

The New Jerusalem and Its Heavenly Doctrine 100

True marriage love is the oneness of two minds, which is a spiritual oneness; and every spiritual oneness comes down from heaven. This is why true marriage love is from heaven and why its primary reality comes from the marriage of the good and the true in heaven . . . .

The pleasure of true marriage love is an inner pleasure because it is a pleasure of minds, and it is also a derivative outer pleasure that is a pleasure of bodies. But the pleasure of a love that is not truly marriage love is only outward, being of bodies but not of minds. This latter pleasure is earthly in quality and almost animal and, therefore, eventually perishes. But the former pleasure is heavenly in quality and human and, therefore, endures.

Arcana Coelestia 10170

There are diversions of charity, which are various activities that bring pleasure and charm to the physical senses, and are useful for mental recreation. . . . A mind that concentrates incessantly on work longs for rest; when it does rest, it comes down into the body and seeks out there pleasures that correspond to its own ways of working. . . . Our more inward physical [natures] draw their gratification primarily from the senses of sight, hearing, smell, taste, and touch. . . . But since our particular tasks, functions, and jobs keep our minds concentrated—and it is our minds that need to be relaxed, revived, and refreshed by these diversions—we can see that the diversions must vary depending on the more inward affection within them. . . .

Charity 189

People who make only a global acknowledgment that they are sinners and call themselves guilty of all evils without exploring themselves (that is, seeing their sins) do make a confession, but not a repentant confession since afterwards they go on living just as they did before.

People who are living lives of faith do their repentance every day, because they reflect on what is wrong with them, identify it, take precautions against it, and ask the Lord for help. We are actually constantly falling, and the Lord is constantly lifting us up. On our own, we fall when we think about intending evil, and we are being lifted up by the Lord when we resist this and, therefore, don't do it. This state is characteristic of everyone who is involved in the good.

Arcana Coelestia 8390–8391

But my friend, avoid evil and do good and believe in the Lord with your whole heart and your whole soul, and the Lord will love you and will give you the love that leads to doing and the faith that leads to believing. Then you will do good out of love and believe out of that faith that is trust; and if you are steadfast in this effort, the result will be that mutual and eternal union that is salvation and eternal life.

True Christian Religion 484

CHAPTER 7

"Correspondence"

.

In one of his summaries of "universal principles," Swedenborg chose to list the "horizontal" relationship between love
and wisdom and the "vertical" relationship between levels of
reality, and then identified "correspondence" as the nature of
this latter relationship. "There is a correspondence between
the elements of the inner person and those of the outer. As a
result, things from either side may appear in different guise, so
different that they may not be recognized unless one is informed about correspondences" (*Heaven and Hell* 356e; see
p. 12 ff).

Correspondence is a theme that runs throughout his theological works. Philosophically, correspondence is the link between spirit and matter, mind and body. Exegetically, it is the
relationship between the literal story of Scripture and a spiritual message within, a subject that will be further developed in
the next chapter. Experientially, it is what connects this physical life with our eternal spiritual life.

It is all too easy to regard the relationship of correspondence as a static one—this spiritual entity "matches" this physical one—but there are clear indications that the relationship is
dynamic. One of Swedenborg's favorite examples is the way a
person's face can express emotions. It is not just that a smile
"corresponds to" a feeling of pleasure; the smile is the effect
of the feeling. When outward things are in their proper "correspondence" to inward ones, he says, "they obey" (*Arcana
Coelestia* 911; see p. 59 ff).

Characteristically, Swedenborg applies this principle in detail. For present purposes, I have selected some of the more general assignments of meaning or identifications of relationship to give accessible examples of correspondence that may suggest their rationale. This is not allegory, in which meanings may be assigned arbitrarily, but an organic relationship based on actual parallels of function. Warmth corresponds to love because it does for the physical world what love does for the spiritual world.

The idea itself has a long history and, perhaps understandably, has received more attention in the arts than in the sciences. In Swedenborg's thought, though, it becomes an essential means to understanding the cosmos as well as ourselves.

General Considerations

There are two lights from which we receive light: the light of the world and the light of heaven. The light of the world comes from the sun; the light of heaven comes from the Lord. The world's light is for the natural or outer person, therefore, for the matters in that person. Even though it may not seem as though these matters belong to that light, they nevertheless do, for nothing can be grasped by the natural person except by means of the kinds of things that occur and appear in this subsolar world. This means they must have some trace of form from the world's light and shade. All the concepts of time, all the concepts of space, so significant to the natural person that thinking would be impossible without them, pertain to this light as well. In contrast, heaven's light is for the spiritual or inner person. Our more inward mind, the locus of concepts we call abstract, is in that light. People are unaware of this even though they refer to their discernment as sight and attribute light to it. This is because, as long as they are involved in worldly and physical concerns, they can perceive only the kinds of things that are proper to the world's light. Heaven's light is from the Lord alone: all heaven is in that light. . . .

Between these lights—or between things in heaven's light and things in the world's light—there is a responsiveness when the outer or natural person is acting as one with the inner or spiritual person: that is, when the former is serving the latter. Then the things that happen in the world's light are portrayals of the kinds of things that happen in heaven's light.

Arcana Coelestia 3223

Everything in the universe is saying something about the Lord's kingdom, so that the universe with its stars, its atmospheres, its three kingdoms is nothing but a kind of theater protraying the heavenly glory of the Lord.

Arcana Coelestia 3000

Each and every thing in nature and its three kingdoms has something active within it from the spiritual world. If there were not this kind [of force] within it, absolutely nothing in the natural world would actuate [the process of] cause and effect, so nothing whatever would result. What is present in natural things from the spiritual world is called the force inherent from first creation, but it is the energy [*conatus*]; when it ceases, action or motion ceases. This is why the whole visible world is a theater that portrays the spiritual world.

Arcana Coelestia 5173:2

THE USES OF ALL CREATED THINGS RISE BY LEVELS FROM THE MOST REMOTE TO HUMAN BEINGS, AND THROUGH HUMAN BEINGS TO GOD THE CREATOR, THEIR SOURCE. *The most remote things*, . . . are all the members of the mineral kingdom—matter in its various forms. . . . *The intermediate things* are all the members of the vegetable kingdom—grasses and herbs of all kinds, shrubs and bushes of all kinds, and trees of all kinds. . . . *The first things* are all the members of the animal kingdom. The lowest ones there are called worms and insects; the intermediate ones, birds and beasts; and the highest, humans.

Divine Love and Wisdom 65

Organic forms are not just the things we can see with our eyes or discover with microscopes; there are also still purer organic forms that are beyond detection either by the naked eye or by artificial means. These forms are more inward. Examples would be forms belonging to our inner sight and then to discernment. These forms are beyond our powers of discovery, but they are still forms—that is, substances.

Arcana Coelestia 4224

We cannot know the difference between these [distinct] levels unless correspondence is known; for these levels are quite distinct from each other, as are a goal, its means, and its result; . . . but they make a one through correspondences.

Doctrine of Sacred Scripture 7

Not many people know what representations and correspondences are, and there is no way they can know unless they are aware that there is a spiritual world distinguishable from the natural world. For correspondences occur between spiritual and natural things, and the things that occur in natural phenomena as a result of spiritual ones are representations. We call them correspondences because they are completely responsive and representations because they portray.

To get some idea of representations and correspondences, we need only reflect on mental processes like thought and intentionality. These usually radiate from the face and are visible in its expression, especially affections, the more inward ones from and in the eyes. When facial [muscles] are acting as one with mental processes, we say they are being responsive ["corresponding"], and the actual expressions themselves portray and are representations.

The same can be said of our bodily motions and of all the actions we accomplish with our muscles. It is recognized that these happen in consequence of what we are thinking and intending. The actual bodily motions and actions portray elements of the mind, and their agreements are correspondences.

Arcana Coelestia 2987–2988

I have learned from heaven that the earliest people had direct revelation, because their more inward reaches were turned toward heaven; and that, as a result, there was a union of the Lord with the human race then. But as time passed, there was not this kind of direct revelation but an indirect one through correspondences. All their divine worship consisted of correspondences, so we call the churches of that era representative churches. They knew what correspondence was and what representation was, and they knew that everything on earth was responsive to spiritual things in heaven and in the church or (which is the same thing) portrayed them. So the natural things that were the outward [forms] of their worship served as means of thinking spiritually, which is thinking with angels.

After knowledge of correspondences and representations had been forgotten, the Word was written, in which all the words and their meanings were correspondences, containing in this way a spiritual or inner meaning that angels are involved in. So when people read the Word and understand it according to its literal or outer meaning, angels are understanding it according to its inner or spiritual meaning. All the thought of angels is, in fact, spiritual, while the thought of people on earth is natural. These thoughts do indeed seem different, but they are one because they correspond.

Heaven and Hell 306

Many people recognize that there is a single substance that is the first and that is the source of everything, but they do not know what this substance is like. They believe that it is so simple that nothing could be simpler, that they can compare it to a point that has no dimensions, and that measurable forms arise from an infinity of points like these.

But this is a fallacy that arises from a spatial concept. Under this kind of concept, the smallest [component] does seem to be like this. The truth is, however, that the simpler and purer anything is, the greater and fuller it is. This is why the more deeply we look into any object, the more wonderful, perfect, and intricate things we see. So, in the first substance of all are the most wonderful, perfect, and intricate things of all. This is because the first substance comes from the spiritual sun, which . . . is from the Lord and in which the Lord dwells. So that sun itself is the single substance of everything and is the greatest and least of created things.

Granted that this sun is the first and single substance, the source of everything, it follows that its contents are infinitely more than can be visible in substances derived from it, which are called substances and, ultimately, matter. The reason all this cannot be visible in them is that they come down from that sun by the two kinds of levels, levels by which all kinds of perfection decrease. This is why, as we have just said, the more deeply we look into anything, the more wonderful, perfect, and intricate things we see.

We have mentioned this to support the proposition that the Divine is in a kind of image in everything that has been created but that it is less and less visible as one comes down by levels—far less when a level separated from the next higher has been closed and blocked off by earthly materials.

Divine Providence 6

"Heaven" in the Word does not in its inner meaning refer to the sky we can see with our eyes but to the Lord's kingdom overall and in detail. If we are focusing on inner matters from outer ones when we look at the sky, we have no thought whatever about a star-studded dome but about the angelic heaven. When we look at the sun, we do not think about the sun but about the Lord as heaven's sun; and it is similar when we look at the moon or the stars. Seeing the vastness of the sky, we do not think about its vastness but about the vast and infinite power of the Lord. It is the same with other things, since there is nothing that is not representative. It is the same with things on our earth. For example, when we see the dawn, we do not think about the dawn but about how all things arise from the Lord and about advancement in the daylight of wisdom. Or again, when we see gardens, groves, and flowerbeds, our eye does not dwell on some particular tree, or its blossom or leaf or fruit, but on the heavenly realities they portray; it does not dwell on the beauty and charm of some particular flower but on the things in the other life that it portrays. For nothing beautiful and charming exists in the heavens or on earth that does not by some relationship portray the Lord's kingdom. . . .

Arcana Coelestia 1807

The earliest people, who lived before the flood, saw some image of and reference to the Lord's kingdom in absolutely everything—in mountains, hills, plains, and valleys, in gardens, groves, and forests, in rivers and lakes, in fields and crops, in all kinds of trees, in all kinds of animals as well, in the luminaries in the sky. . . .

Arcana Coelestia 2722:5

I have been taught by an abundance of experience that there is not the slightest thing in the natural world, in its three kingdoms, that does not portray something in the spiritual world or that does not have something there to which it is responsive. . . .

Arcana Coelestia 2992

Correspondences in Nature

The most universal principle is that the Lord is heaven's sun and is the source of all light in the other life. To angels and spirits (or to people in the other life), nothing whatever of the world's light is visible—the world's light, which comes from the sun, is nothing but profound darkness to angels. From heaven's sun or the Lord there comes not only light but warmth as well, but the light is spiritual and the warmth is spiritual. To the eyes of spiritual beings, the light looks like light; but because of its source, it contains intelligence and wisdom. By the senses of spiritual beings, the warmth is perceived as warmth; but because of its source, there is love within it. So too love is called spiritual warmth and causes the warmth of human life, and intelligence is called spiritual light and causes the light of human life. From this universal correspondence flows the rest. For each and every reality goes back

91

to the good, which is a matter of love, and the true, which is a matter of intelligence.

Arcana Coelestia 3636

In the inner meaning, the sun refers to the Lord and secondarily, therefore, to heavenly [qualities] of love and compassion, especially to love and compassion themselves. . . . So we can see that "sunset" is the last time of the church, called its consummation, when there is no longer any compassion. The Lord's church is like the times of day—its first age like sunrise and morning, its last like sunset or evening and darkness. . . .

Arcana Coelestia 1837

[T]he sun refers to love for the Lord and compassion toward the neighbor; the moon, to the faith appropriate to that love and compassion; and the stars, to insights into what is good and true. . . .

Arcana Coelestia 2495:2

The reason that morning refers to [a state of enlightenment] is that all the times of day, like all the seasons of the year, refer to different states according to differences in heaven's light. The changes in heaven's light are not like the daily and yearly changes of light in this world but are changes in intelligence and love. For heaven's light is simply divine intelligence from the Lord, which is luminous to [angels'] senses; and the warmth of that light is the Lord's divine love, which is correspondingly warm to their senses. This light is what causes human discernment, and this warmth is what causes our vital warmth and our ability to intend what is good. Morning or dawn, there is a state of enlightenment, especially as to what is good and true, which arises when it is recognized and increases when it is perceived that the good is actually good and the true true. Perception is an inner revelation, so morning refers to what is revealed; and since what has been obscure then becomes clear, morning also refers to clarity. Primarily, in the highest sense, morning refers to the Lord him-

self, because the Lord is the sun from which comes all the
light in heaven. . . .

Arcana Coelestia 5097

Faith without love is like the sun's light without its warmth,
as in winter when nothing grows but everything lies dormant
or dies. In contrast, faith together with love is like the sun's
light in springtime when everything grows and blooms.

Arcana Coelestia 34:2

"[A] cloud" is used to mean an obscure form of what is true
and, more precisely, the literal meaning of the Word since this
meaning, relative to the inner meaning, is an obscure form of
what is true. . . .

Arcana Coelestia 8106:2

All earthly things can be distinguished into three general
classes called kingdoms: namely, the animal kingdom, the vegetable kingdom, and the mineral kingdom. The members of
the animal kingdom are correspondences in the first level because they are alive. The members of the vegetable kingdom
are correspondences in the second level because they only
grow. The members of the mineral kingdom are correspondences in the third level because they neither live nor grow.

Heaven and Hell 104

Both larger and smaller animals refer to characteristic affections, or things that can be traced back to our intentionality;
or they mean characteristic thoughts, or things that can be
traced back to our discernment. . . . Both walking and creep-
ing animals refer to affections in either sense, good or bad,
since these are matters of affection, while the flying animals
and insects refer to characteristic thoughts in either sense, true
or false, since these are matters of thought.

Arcana Coelestia 9331

When angels are involved in affections and are at the same
time talking about them, these matters descend into the lower

realm among spirits in kinds of portrayals of animals. When the talk is of good affections, beautiful animals are presented, gentle and useful, the kinds used for sacrifices in symbolic divine worship in the Jewish church, such as lambs, sheep, kids, she-goats, rams, male calves, young bulls, and cattle. Then something more appears over the animal, presenting some image of their thought, and upright spirits are granted a perception of it. This assures us of the meaning of the animals in the rituals of the Jewish church and of the same animals mentioned [elsewhere] in the Word—affections.

Arcana Coelestia 3218

When angels are talking together about insights, concepts, and inflow, then there appear in the world of spirits birds that seem to be formed to accord with the topic of their conversation. This is why birds in the Word mean rational matters or matters of thought. . . .

Arcana Coelestia 3219

[T]rees in general refer to perceptions and insights—perceptions when the subject is a heavenly person but insights when the subject is a spiritual person. . . .

Arcana Coelestia 4013:3

A person who is being reborn, like a tree, begins from a seed; so "seed" is used in the Word to refer to the true that comes from the good. Then, just like a tree, the individual produces leaves; and, then, flowers; and, eventually, fruit. The person produces elements of understanding, which are referred to in the Word as "leaves," and then elements of wisdom. These are referred to as "flowers." Finally, the person brings forth elements of life, namely, good things of love and compassion in act, which in the Word are referred to as "fruits." This kind of pictorial resemblance between a fruit tree and a person who is being regenerated is so complete that one can learn from a tree how regeneration works, given only some prior knowledge of what is spiritually good and true.

Arcana Coelestia 5115:2

"[W]aters" refer to insights and data . . . and "seas," therefore, to gatherings of such things.

Arcana Coelestia 28

"[S]oil" [*humus*] refers to the outer person. . . . When someone has been regenerated, then that individual is no longer called "land" [*terra*] but "soil," because heavenly seeds have been planted there. We are compared to soil and called soil throughout the Word. It is the outer person, or its affection and memory, where the seeds of the good and the true are planted, not the inner person, since, in the inner, there is nothing that really belongs to us, only in the outer. In the inner, there are things good and true that do not seem to be there as long as we are [centered] in what is outward and physical. Still, the Lord stores them away in the internal, unknown to us, since they do not emerge until the outer person apparently dies, usually in times of temptation-trials, misfortune, sickness, or on the deathbed.

Arcana Coelestia 268

Correspondences in the Human Form

There are outside forces acting [on the human body] that are forces of nature and are not intrinsically alive; and there are inside forces acting that are intrinsically alive. These hold every entity together and enable it to live, depending on the form granted it for the sake of its use.

Not many people believe that this this true, the reason being that they do not know what the spiritual is and what the natural is, let alone how they are to be distinguished. Nor do they know what correspondence is or what inflow is or that, when the spiritual flows into the body's organic forms, it sets up the kinds of life process that we observe. Nor do they know that without this kind of inflow and responsiveness, not the smallest particle of the body would be able to possess life and be moved. As to how this happens, I have been taught by live experience that not only does heaven flow in a general way, but [heavenly] communities flow into this or that organ of the body and into this or that member. I have also been taught that it is not just one community that flows into a given organ or member but many, and that there are many individuals in each community. For the more there are, the better and stronger is the responsiveness, since perfection and strength come from a harmonious gathering of many constituents that act as one in a heavenly form. So the impulse that reflects in specific instances is more perfect and stronger depending on the abundance of constituents.

As a result, I have been able to determine that the particular viscera and members, or motor and sensory organs, are responsive to communities in heaven exactly as though they were distinct heavens, and that from them (that is, through them) heavenly and spiritual forces flow into people. They flow into forms that are both sufficient and suitable and, in this way, set up the results that people observe. But to human beings, these results seem to be entirely matters of nature—that is, in a completely different form and in another guise, so different that there is no way to recognize that they are coming from a spiritual source.

Arcana Coelestia 3628

There are two things in the human body that are the well-springs of all motion, of all action and sensation of the outer body, the body alone. These are the heart and the lungs. These answer to the universal human or heaven of the Lord in a particular fashion, by virtue of the fact that heavenly angels there make one kingdom; and spiritual angels, a second one, the Lord's kingdom being heavenly and spiritual. The heavenly kingdom consists of people who are involved in love to the Lord; the spiritual kingdom, of people who are involved in compassion toward the neighbor. . . . The heart, and its kingdom in the human being, answers to heavenly matters; the lungs, and their kingdom, answer to spiritual matters. Further, these so flow into elements of the heart and the lungs that these latter actually come into being and are maintained by that inflow.

Arcana Coelestia 3635

96

In the other life, we are not nourished by any natural food and drink but by spiritual food and drink. Spiritual food is the good, and spiritual drink is the true. So where bread or food are mentioned in the Word, angels understand spiritual bread or food—the good of love and compassion; and where water or drink are mentioned, they understand spiritual water or drink—what is true of faith.

Arcana Coelestia 4976

Heaven's form is awesome and utterly surpasses all human understanding. It is, in fact, far loftier than any concepts of form that anyone can possibly grasp even by analysis of earthly matters. All the heavenly communities are arranged according to this form. And marvelous as it is, there is an orbiting according to the forms, which angels and spirits do not feel. It is like the earth's daily rotation on its axis and annual orbit of the sun, which its inhabitants do not notice.

Arcana Coelestia 4041

The five outer senses—touch, taste, smell, hearing, and sight—have specific correspondences with inner senses; but these correspondences are virtually unknown nowadays because hardly anyone knows that any correspondences exist, let alone that there are correspondences of spiritual realities with natural ones or of elements of the inner person with elements of the outer, which is the same thing.

On the correspondence of the senses, the sense of touch corresponds in general to affection for what is good; the sense of taste, to affection for knowing; the sense of smell, to affection for perceiving; the sense of hearing, to affection for learning and to obedience; and the sense of sight, to affection for discerning and being wise.

Arcana Coelestia 4404

The people in the universal human who correspond to the hands, arms, and also the shoulders are the ones possessed of power through faith's truth derived from what is good. . . .

Arcana Coelestia 4932

The people in the universal human who correspond to the feet, soles, and heels are people who are nature-centered; so "feet" are used in the Word to indicate things of nature; . . . and "soles," lower elements of nature. . . . Actually, heavenly things in the universal human constitute the head; spiritual things, the body; and natural things, the feet.

Arcana Coelestia 4938

[D]iseases too have a correspondence with the spiritual world. It is not a correspondence with heaven, the universal human, but with people in its opposite, with people in the hells. By "the spiritual world" in the broadest sense, we mean heaven and hell. When people die, they cross from the natural world into the spiritual world.

The reason diseases have their correspondence with these people is that diseases correspond to cravings and passions of the spirit (*animi*), these being their source. In general, the sources of diseases are excess, various kinds of extravagance, pleasures merely physical, and also hatred, vengefulness, licentiousness, and the like. These are destructive of people's inner reaches; and as these are destroyed, the more outward elements are affected, bringing people into disease, and by disease to death. . . .

This does not, however, hinder people from being healed by means on the natural level. This is actually in harmony with the means of divine providence.

Arcana Coelestia 5712

[I]f people had lived good lives, then their more inward elements would be open to heaven, and through heaven to the Lord; . . . so people would be free of disease. There would be only a decline in extreme old age, when they became children again but wise children. And then when the body could no longer serve the inner person, the spirit, people would cross without illness from their earthly bodies into the kind of bodies angels have—straight from the world into heaven.

Arcana Coelestia 5726

98

CHAPTER 8

Revelation

·

Revelation may well be one of the most controversial topics in the field of religion. It conjures up visions—or nightmares—of absolute dogmatism, of claims to infallibility, and of all the intolerance and repression that such attitudes have engendered in the past. Yet, on the other hand, there would seem little point to a deity who did not communicate with us.

There is material in each of the preceding chapters that contributes to a Swedenborgian resolution of this dilemma. The first chapter gave reason for us to be wary of claiming any kind of perfect understanding. The second chapter proposed that the Divine, including all meaning, was everywhere present. The third chapter viewed the world in which we are engaged as a particularly dim and sluggish reflection of the lucid world of spirit. The fourth and fifth chapters presented us as beings both with limitations and in process, beings to whom freedom and rationality are central; and the sixth chapter touched on the interaction between the values we choose to live by and the depth of our understanding. Finally, the seventh chapter dealt with the way in which the physical world images the spiritual world.

The only kind of revelation consistent with these concepts would be both universal and ambiguous—universal because of Divine omnipresence and ambiguous because of the importance of our freedom and rationality. These premises could not tolerate any "revelation" that compelled belief or overrode our freedom. They could not tolerate any "revelation" that privileged one group of people over others or, to put it negatively, that barred some people from salvation through no fault of their own.

At the same time, there is no question that, for Swedenborg, the Judaeo-Christian Scriptures are normative. This is consistent with his universalism, I would suggest, because he regards them as the most perfect or complete *precis* of the way or ways in which the Divine is communicating with everyone everywhere all the time. Certainly, possessing Scripture is no guarantee of special favor. Quite the contrary, familiarity with them brings with it a special measure of accountability; and, in Swedenborg's view, Christians have quite persistently and spectacularly failed to live up to their revelation.

This view is involved in a broader view of the spiritual history of humanity, according to which we have regularly failed to heed the guidance given and have, therefore, fallen to new "lows," and the Divine has regularly reached out us on whatever level we have chosen to live. This leads to a sweeping periodization of history reminiscent of widespread mythological views but embedded in a much more contemporary and subtle understanding of human nature.

Personal Revelation

The people of the earliest church got their insights into true faith by revelations, since they talked with the Lord and with angels and were taught through visions and dreams that they found utterly delightful and heavenly [*paradisiaca*]. They had a constant perceptiveness from the Lord, such a perceptiveness that, when they thought from the contents of their memory they instantly perceived whether their thinking was true or not. This was so reliable that, when anything false intruded, they were not only repelled, they were horrified. The state of angels is like this as well. But the earliest church's perceptiveness was later replaced by insight into what is true and good, first through revelation and eventually through things revealed in the Word.

Arcana Coelestia 125

There is a light of heaven and a light of the world, the light of heaven for our spirit and the light of the world for our body. It works like this: what we can see in heaven's light is in darkness when we are seeing in the world's light; and, vice versa, what we can see in the world's light is in darkness when we are seeing in heaven's light. This means that, when our physical eyes are deprived of the world's light, the eyes of our spirit are opened and we see what heaven's light discloses.

Arcana Coelestia 9577

When internal breathing* ceased, an external breathing gradually supplanted it, much like modern breathing; and along with this external breathing came verbal speech or the articulation of sound in which deeper concepts of thought are given boundaries. So the human state was completely changed and became such that people could no longer have that kind of perception. Instead of perception, they had a kind of inner voice [*dictamen*] that could be called conscience. For it was like conscience, even though it was halfway between perception and the conscience some people recognize in our times. Further, once this kind of limiting of thought concepts (by verbal speech, that is) had happened, they could no longer be taught through the inner person like the earliest people but [only] through the outer. So the earliest church's revelations were replaced by doctrinal [processes] that were first apprehended by the outer senses and from which substantial memory concepts; and then thought concepts might be formed as means and guides to their learning.

Arcana Coelestia 608

[P]eople who are involved in what is good and, therefore, in what is true (especially people who are involved in the good of love to the Lord) have a revelation from perception, while people who are not involved in what is good and, therefore, in what is true can actually have revelation but not from percep-

*Swedenborg reports having experimented as a child with minimal breathing as an aid to prayer and of experiencing suspension of breathing during periods of intense concentration as an adult. He states that such "internal breathing" was characteristic of the earliest humans.

tion. It can happen through a direct voice that they hear
within themselves, which means through angels from the
Lord. This kind of revelation is external, while the former is
internal . . . . Nowadays, . . . quite a few people have verbal
revelations apart from any perception, even people who are
not involved in anything good, especially through dreams or
visions . . . . But since these people lack perception, they are
only verbal or visual revelations without any perception of
their meaning. Genuine perceptiveness arises through heaven
from the Lord and influences a person's intellect spiritually,
leading it observably toward thinking in accord with reality,
with an inner agreement from some unidentified source. It
seems to be inherent in the person, but it is an inner voice
through heaven from the Lord flowing into the deeper levels
of thought, concerned with matters that transcend the natural
and the sensory—that is, matters involving the spiritual world
and heaven.

Arcana Coelestia   5121:2–3

Prayer, seen in its own right, is talking with God, with a consequent inner insight into the contents of the prayer. There
comes in response to this something like an inflow into the
mind's perception or thought, as though there were a kind of
opening of our inner reaches toward God. But this varies with
our state and with the essential nature of the prayer. If it comes
from love and faith and if only heavenly and spiritual matters
are prayed about and for, then there occurs in the prayer something like a revelation, which is sensed in the affection of the
person as hope, solace, or a kind of inner rejoicing. This is why
prayer in its inner meaning refers to revelation.

Arcana Coelestia   2535

Epochal Revelations

In regard to the Word in particular, there has always been one
but not [always] the Word we have today. There was a different Word in the earliest church that existed before the flood,
and a different one again in the early church that existed after

102

the flood. But our Word was written by Moses and the prophets in the Jewish church and then by the evangelists in a new church. The reason there has always been a Word is that, through the Word, there is a communication of heaven with earth and that the Word deals with what is good and true so that people can live happily to eternity. So too, in its inner meaning, it deals solely with the Lord because he is the source of everything that is good and true.

The Word in the earliest church . . . was not a written Word but was revealed to every individual who was of [literally, "from"] the church. They were actually heavenly people, involved, therefore, in a perception of what was good and true like the angels with whom they kept company. So they had the Word written on their hearts. . . . Since they were heavenly people and kept company with angels, everything they saw they took in a particular meaning, as symbolic and indicative of heavenly and spiritual matters. . . .

Arcana Coelestia 2895–2896

When a church has been so laid waste that there is no longer any faith [in it], then and only then is there a new beginning, or a new light shining forth, which is called "a morning."

Arcana Coelestia 408

The Word in the early church that existed after the flood, though, was derived [from the former one]. Since the people of that church were spiritual but not heavenly, they knew what the symbols and signs meant but did not grasp the meaning by perception. Since the symbols and signs enfolded divine matters, they observed them in practice and used them in divine worship. This happened so that they would have a communication with heaven.

Arcana Coelestia 2897

[A]s time passed, wisdom retreated from very inward realms to very outward ones, and people moved away from heaven. Eventually, they came all the way down to the dust of the earth, where they now place wisdom.

Arcana Coelestia 3432:3

103

The Judaeo-Christian Scriptures

What is divine is beyond comprehension, since it is above all discernment, even the angelic. Still, this divine, incomprehensible in itself, can flow into human rationality through the Divine-Human; and when it does flow into our rationality, it is accepted there according to the truths already there—variously, that is, in different people. The more genuine the truths within us, the more perfectly we accept the divine that is flowing in, and the more our discernment is enlightened. In the Lord's Word, there are actual truths; but in its literal meaning, there are truths that have been adapted to the grasp of people who are involved in outward worship. In its inner meaning, however, there are truths adapted to people who are "inner people," who in both doctrine and life are angelic, that is.

Arcana Coelestia 2531:2

In the earliest times, there was no Word, but there was a direct revelation to the people of the church; and through it, there was a union. For when there is direct revelation, then there is a union of heaven with mortals. The union of heaven with mortals is a union of the Lord with them, since the Lord's Divine among angels constitutes heaven.

When this direct revelation ceased (which happened when people turned aside from the good they had been involved in), then another revelation took its place, a revelation through symbols that enabled people to know what was true and good. This church was, therefore, called a symbolic church. There was also a Word in that church but one useful only to that church. When that church too had been laid waste (which happened when they began to idolize the symbols through which the church was then united with heaven and, in many lands, to turn them to magical uses), then it was provided by the Lord that a Word should be written that would be divine in every detail, even in every least word, and that would be composed of pure correspondences. In this way, it would be adapted to the perception of angels in all the heavens and at the same time to mortals. The purpose of this was to maintain the union of the Lord with the human race.

Arcana Coelestia   10632:3–4

I have talked with some spirits about the Word, on the necessity that some revelation, by the Lord's divine providence, should have arisen. For revelation or the Word is a general vessel recipient of spiritual and heavenly things and, thereby, uniting heaven and earth.

Arcana Coelestia   1775

I have been told by angels that the Lord's Word is a dead letter but that, while it is being read, it is brought to life by the Lord in accord with each individual's ability. It comes to life according to [one's] life of compassion and state of innocence, with immeasurable variety.

Arcana Coelestia   1776

I have talked with good spirits about the fact that many things in the Word—more than anyone could believe—are written acording to appearances and according to sensory deceptions, such as statements that Jehovah is in blazing wrath and rage against the ungodly, that he rejoices over their ruin, that he even kills them. Things like this are said so that people's pet opinions [*persuasiones*] will not be shattered but will be deflected. For talking contrary to someone's grasp of things (a grasp made up of appearances, deceptive notions, and pet opinions) would be sowing seed in water and saying things that would immediately be rejected. Still, these [appearances in the Word] can serve as general vessels containing spiritual and heavenly things, since these, being all from the Lord, can be instilled into them.

Arcana Coelestia   1874

Divine truth such as the Word is pleasing in its outward form or literal meaning because, by interpretations, it is susceptible of being explained in favor of anyone. This is not true of its inner meaning, though.

Arcana Coelestia   5620:13

It is recognized that there are many people in the church who are influenced by the Lord's Word and devote a great deal of labor to reading it. But there are few who do so with a view to being taught about the truth. Most of them actually stay within their own dogma and just work to confirm it from the Word. They seem to be involved in an affection for the truth, but they are not. The only people who are involved in an affection for the truth are those who love to be taught about what is true, that is, to know what is true, and who search the scriptures with this end in view. No one is involved in this affection except those who are involved in what is good—that is, in compassion toward the neighbor—and even more so those who are in a love for the Lord. For them, the good itself is flowing into the true and producing the affection, since the Lord is present in that good.

Arcana Coelestia 4368:2

The Word is said to be closed when it is understood only in its literal meaning and everything there is taken as doctrine. It is still more closed when those elements that favor the desires of love of self and the world are taken as doctrine, since these elements especially roll a great stone over the mouth of the well.

Arcana Coelestia 3769

A doctrine of genuine truth can be fully drawn from the literal meaning of the Word. For in this meaning, the Word is like a person clothed, with hands and face bare. All the things essential to our life (that is, to our salvation) are bare, but the rest are clothed; and in many places where they are clothed, they shine through the way a face shines through a thin veil. The truths of the Word are also multiplied by being loved. As they are arranged in order by love, they shine and appear more and more clearly through their garments.

Four Doctrines, "The Doctrine of Sacred Scripture" 55

The Word is divine primarily because each and every detail is not focused on a single nation or a single people, but on the whole human race—on what has been and what is and what is to be. In a more inclusive sense, it focuses on the Lord's kingdom in the heavens; and in its highest sense, it focuses on the Lord himself. This is what makes the Word divine.

Arcana Coelestia 3305:2

The contents of this chapter [Genesis 14] do not seem to be symbolic, since they deal simply with wars among a number of kings, Lot's rescue by Abraham, and finally with Melchizedek, exactly as though there were no heavenly treasure hidden within. Nevertheless, here as everywhere else there are the most profound secrets [*arcana*] stored away in the inner meaning, which also follow in unbroken sequence from the matters that precede and are connected in unbroken sequence with the things that follow.

Arcana Coelestia 1659

People who keep their minds focused solely on historical concerns know only that these words [Genesis 25:24–26] and those preceding foretell things that would happen between Esau and Jacob and are confirmed in this opinion by the narration that follows. But the Lord's Word is such that historical matters are in their sequence and spiritual matters (which are matters of spiritual meaning) in theirs. The former focus on the outer person but the latter, on the inner; and so there is a correspondence between the two, the outer person and the inner. This is accomplished by the Word, the Word being, in fact, a coming together of heaven and earth, as we have often presented. So in every individual who reads the Word in holiness, there is a coming together of his or her outer person that is on earth with his or her inner person that is in heaven.

Arcana Coelestia 3304:3

People who believe that the holy Divine in the Word lies no more hidden than the meaning discernible in the letter see . . . [the Word's] holiness only from a faith that everything there has been divinely inspired and that it contains inexplicable secrets known only to God. . . . Let them know that the holy Divine is hidden in each and every detail of the Word, but it rests in the fact that everything there deals with the Lord and with his kingdom and church. . . .

Arcana Coelestia   9086:3

The nature of the inner meaning is such that the actual affection latent in the words is what constitutes the inner meaning. . . .

Arcana Coelestia   1492

The Word in its spiritual meaning deals solely with matters of the Lord and the neighbor—that is, with matters of love to the Lord and toward the neighbor—which is why the Word is alive. This is what is meant by saying that the Law and the prophets hang on these two commandments (Matthew 22:38), the Law and the prophets being the entire Word taken as a whole.

Arcana Coelestia   9841:4

In the original language, one series is not marked off from another by punctuation marks as in other languages, but they look like a continuum from beginning to end. The contents of the inner meaning actually have a similar continuity, flowing from one state of affairs into another; but when one state ends and another takes its place, this is indicated [by distinctive words]. . . .

Arcana Coelestia   4987

The resting of the ark [Genesis 8:4] indicates regeneration. . . . When the ark is said to come to rest, it is [in reference to] a person's regeneration. We càn see what is involved from the sequence of the literal meaning, namely, that the resting of the ark indicates that the fluctuations after a temptation-trial have ceased. But the fluctuations, which are doubts and obscurities about what is true and good, do not cease like this. They last a long time, as we must conclude from what is to follow. This demonstrates that things are constantly different in the inner meaning.

Having doctrinal tenets based on the Word does not mean that these tenets are divine truths, since all kinds of doctrine can be gotten from the Word—false ones as readily as true. . . . But this does not happen if the doctrine is formed by the inner meaning. The inner meaning is not just the meaning hidden within the outer meaning, as already presented, but is also that meaning that results from an abundance of instances of literal meaning appropriately gathered and observed by people who have been mentally enlightened by the Lord. . . . But a mind cannot be enlightened apart from a belief that love to the Lord and compassion toward the neighbor are the first and foremost principles of the church. People who proceed from an acknowledgment of these principles, if they abide within them, see countless truths, an abundance of hidden things disclosed, from an inner recognition that depends on their level of enlightenment by the Lord.

Arcana Coelestia 7233:3

The Word is like a divine person: the literal meaning is like its body, and the inner meaning is like its soul. So we can see that the literal meaning lives because of the inner meaning. It does seem as though the literal meaning would vanish or die because of the inner meaning, but the opposite is the case. It does not vanish, much less die, but comes to life because of the inner meaning.

Arcana Coelestia 8943

[T]he literal meaning of the Word would have been different if the Word had been composed among a different people or if this people had been of a different character. After all, the Word's literal meaning does deal with this people because the Word was composed in their community.

Arcana Coelestia 10453:3

There is a still deeper meaning in the Word, which is called heavenly, . . . but this meaning is almost impossible to unfold because it falls less into the thought of discernment than into the affection of intentionality.

The Four Doctrines, "The Doctrine of Sacred Scripture" 19

We can see the holiness of the Word (and the special holiness in its deeper levels) quite clearly from the fact that there is a heavenly marriage in its details—a marriage of the good and the true; and, therefore, a heaven. We can see its holiness also from the fact that, in its deeper levels, there is a marriage of the Lord's Divine-Human with his kingdom and church and, in fact, in the highest meaning a uniting in the Lord of his intrinsic Divine and his Divine-Human.

Arcana Coelestia 6343:2

[T]he Word in its inmost and highest meaning is about the Lord alone and especially about the glorifying of his human [nature].

Arcana Coelestia 9389

CHAPTER 9

The Community of the Spirit

.

When Swedenborg identifies as the purpose of heaven the formation of a heaven from the human race, this should alert us to the importance of community in his thought. While there is a vital strand of individualism in his theology in that the salvation of each single person depends on the character formed by the decisions that individual makes, there is never any doubt that these decisions are made in the context of relationships. In fact, their quality, and the quality of the character they form, is determined primarily by the effect they have on human relationships.

The human cosmos sketched in the material selected for the preceding chapters is an intensively interactive cosmos. There is no such thing as an "isolated" individual. We are designed and created to live in community, and the whole effort of the Divine, through revelation and through the subtler workings of providence, is to keep open to us paths that lead to the growth of perceptive and loving communities. In this view, the resolution of inner conflicts (the struggles mentioned in the chapter on the human process) and the resolution of outer conflicts are different sides of the same coin.

The church, then, exists solely for the purpose of supporting the processes that nurture heavenly community. These are the processes of individual spiritual growth and of thoughtful and loving human interaction. There is no magical benefit to worship: it is of value as it strengthens the understanding of

111

and will to heavenly community. There is no automatic equation between church membership and salvation. As noted earlier, our acceptance into heaven depends on our internalization of heavenly qualities, our acceptance of heaven into ourselves.

The Nature of Spiritual Community

All the people in heaven find companionship according to spiritual affinities, which are affinities of the good and the true in their own pattern; this holds true for heaven as a whole in each community and in each household. This is why angels who are involved in similar kinds of the good and the true recognize each other the way relatives and friends do on earth, just as though they had known each other from infancy.

There is a similar gathering of the good and true elements that make up wisdom and intelligence in each individual angel. They recognize each other in the same way, and as they recognize each other, they unite.

Heaven and Hell 205

Since love is the source of human life and since the quality of a person's love determines the quality of the whole person and since love is spiritual union, it, therefore, follows that all people in the other life find companionship according to their loves. . . .

Arcana Coelestia 7085

Heavenly companionships depend on people's lives, never on thoughts that are not matters of life. Thoughts that are not matters of life are pretenses that are wholly cast aside.

Arcana Coelestia 2228:2

I have been allowed to talk with some people in the other life who had withdrawn from the world's affairs in order to live in piety and sanctity and also with some people who had punished themselves in various ways, in the belief that this was renouncing the world and taming the desires of the flesh. But most of them, since they had by this means adopted a joyless lifestyle and withdrawn from a life of compassion (a life that can be led only in involvement in the world), were unable to be in the company of angels, since the life of angels is happy because of their blessedness and consists of performing those good acts that are works of compassion.

Heaven and Hell 535

I have talked with some people after death who, during their lives on earth, had renounced the world and had dedicated themselves to virtually solitary lives, in order, by withdrawing their thoughts from worldly matters, to free themselves for pious meditations. They believed that this was following the way to heaven. But in the other life, these people have joyless dispositions; they avoid other people who are not like themselves, they feel insulted because their lot is not happier than others' because they think they deserve better, they do not care about other people, and they avoid the duties of compassion that unite people with heaven.

Heaven and Hell 360

To prevent people from being in heaven as to discernment and in hell as to intentionality, thereby having their minds divided, all discernment that transcends a person's very own love is taken away after death. As a result, intentionality and discernment ultimately make one in all people. In people who are in heaven, the intentionality loves what is good and the discernment thinks what is true, while, in people who are in hell, the intentionality loves what is evil and the discernment thinks what is false. The same thing happens in this world when someone is thinking from his or her own spirit, which happens in solitude, even though many people think differently when they are in public.

Divine Love and Wisdom 397

We can determine the greatness of heaven's joy from the fact that all the people there find their own joy in sharing their joy and blessedness with someone else. Since everyone in the heavens is like this, we can see how great heaven's joy is.

Heaven and Hell   399

Ecclesiastical Pluralism

Provision has been made by the Lord that there should be some form of religion almost everywhere; and provision has also been made by the Lord that everyone who acknowledges God and does not do wrong because it is against God should have a place in heaven. Heaven, taken all together, reflects a single person, whose life or soul is the Lord. In that heavenly person are all the components that exist in the natural person, the difference being like that between what is heavenly and what is natural. . . .

That heavenly person . . . cannot be made up of the people of one religion—it needs people of many religions. So everyone who has made these two universal [principles] of the church matters of life has a place in that heavenly person—that is, in heaven.

Divine Providence   326:9–10

It is a matter of the Lord's divine providence that every nation should have some religion, and every nation that lives its religion (that is, that does not do wrong because it is against their God) receives something spiritual in its natural.

If you were to hear some gentile refusing to do this or that wrong because it was against his or her God, would you not say inside, "Isn't this person saved? It seems inevitable." Sound reason demands it. And on the other hand, suppose you were to hear a Christian say, "This or that wrong doesn't matter at all. What is this business about its being against God?" Would you not say inside, "Is this person saved? It seems impossible." This, too, sound reason demands.

If this individual were to say, "I was born a Christian, I have been baptized, I acknowledge the Lord, read the Word, and take communion," do these things matter when there is a breathing aura of murders and acts of revenge, of acts of adultery, false witness, theft, and violence, and these are not taken to be sins? Is a person like that thinking about God or about eternal life? Does a person like that think that God and eternal life exist? Doesn't sound reason demand that such a person cannot be saved?

We make these statements about Christians because gentiles, from their religion, think about God in their lives more than Christians do.

Divine Providence 322:4–5

Whenever a religion is sown, the Lord's leading of its people is in accord with its rules and tenets, and the Lord provides that every religion shall have rules like those in the Ten Commandments—requiring, for example, the worship of God, not taking God's name lightly, observing holy days, respecting parents, and not killing, committing adultery, stealing, or perjuring oneself.

Divine Providence 254:2

The churches before the Lord's coming were all symbolic [*repraesentativae*] churches. The Israelite church was like this. The tabernacle, Aaron's vestments, the sacrifices, everything about the temple in Jerusalem, and even their laws were symbolic. Among the early people, the knowledge of correspondences (which is also the knowledge of symbols) was the essential knowledge of the wise, especially developed in Egypt, where it gave rise to hieroglyphics.

They knew from this information the meanings of all kinds of animals and all kinds of trees; the meanings of mountains and hills, rivers, springs; of the sun, moon, and stars; and since all their worship was symbolic, made up wholly of correspondences, they held their worship on mountains and hills and also in groves and gardens. For the same reason they regarded springs as holy and faced the east in their worship of God. We note particularly that they made statues of horses, cattle, calves, sheep, even birds, fish, and serpents; and placed them in their homes arranged according to the spiritual [values] of

115

their church to which they corresponded or which they symbolized. They also placed them in their temples as reminders, to summon the holy things they referred to.

In later times, when the knowledge of correspondences had been forgotten, their descendants began to worship the statues themselves as intrinsically holy, unaware that their forebears had not seen anything holy in them but that the statues had by their correspondences simply symbolized and, therefore, pointed to holy things. So an idolatry arose that filled the whole sphere of lands—Asia and its surrounding islands as well as Africa and Europe.

To uproot all these forms of idolatry, it happened under divine providence that a new religion of an eastern type began, in which there was something from both Testaments of the Word, and that taught that the Lord had come into the world and was the greatest prophet, the wisest of all, and the son of God. This was done through Muhammad. . . .

Divine Providence 255:2–3

Unity and Distinction

Disagreement in matters of doctrine does not prevent a church from being united if only there is a unanimity about willing well and acting well.

Arcana Coelestia 3451:2

There is a single doctrine when all people have mutual love or compassion. Mutual love and compassion make them one, even though they are different, since a one is made up of different components. All [such] people, no matter how many (even to hundreds of thousands), if they are involved in compassion or mutual love, have a single goal, namely, the common good, the Lord's kingdom, and the Lord himself. Differences in doctrine and worship are then like the differences between the senses and organs in a person, which contribute to the perfection of the whole. Then the Lord flows in and works through compassion uniquely for everyone's individuality and arranges the entire group in a pattern—on earth, therefore, as in heaven; and then the Lord's will, as the Lord himself teaches, is done on earth as in heaven.

Arcana Coelestia 1285:3

What makes heaven in a person also makes the church, since the church is the Lord's heaven on earth. . . .

We define the church as being where the Lord is recognized and where the Word is present, since the essentials of the church are the Lord's gifts of love and faith in the Lord and the Word teaches how we must live in order to accept love and faith from the Lord.

The Lord's church exists in internal and external forms. The internal church is in people who do the Lord's commandments from love since these are the people who love the Lord. The external church is in people who do the Lord's commandments from faith since these are the people who believe in the Lord.

For this church to exist, there must be doctrine from the Word since, without doctrine, the Word is unintelligible. But doctrine alone in a person does not constitute the church; it takes a life in accord with the doctrine. It follows from this that faith alone does not make the church but the life of faith, which is compassion.

The real doctrine of the church is a doctrine of compassion and faith together and not a doctrine of faith without one of compassion. For a doctrine of compassion and faith together is a doctrine of life, but a doctrine of faith without a doctrine of compassion is not.

People who are outside this church and who still recognize a single deity and live their religion in some form of compassion toward the neighbor are in communion with people in the church since no one who believes in God and lives well is damned. So we can see that the Lord's church is everywhere in the whole world, though it exists in its particular form where the Lord is recognized and where the Word is present.

Arcana Coelestia 10760–10765

In Christendom, it is doctrinal matters that set churches apart and that result in people calling themselves Roman

117

Catholics, Lutherans, Calvinists, and so on. These names stem entirely from doctrine and would never have happened if people had made love to the Lord and compassion toward the neighbor the main point of faith. Then these [doctrinal] things would have been only varieties of opinion about the mysteries of faith, which true Christians would leave to everyone according to his or her conscience; and they would have said at heart that a true Christian is a person who lives like a Christian or who lives as the Lord teaches. In this way, one church would have come into being from all the different ones, and all the dissension that results from doctrine alone would have vanished. In fact, the hatred of one group against another would have evaporated immediately, and the Lord's kingdom would have been on earth.

Arcana Coelestia   1799:4

Functions of the Church

As for the clergy [*sacerdotes*], they are to teach people the way to heaven and also to lead them. They are to teach them according to the doctrine of their own church and lead them so that they live by it. . . .

The clergy are to claim no power over people's souls because they do not know the state of others' deeper reaches. Much less are they to claim the power of opening or closing heaven since this power belongs to the Lord alone. . . .

The clergy are to have respect and honor because of the holy offices they serve, but the wise ones give this honor to the Lord, who is the source of holiness, and not to themselves. . . .

The clergy are to teach people and lead them by truths to goodness of life, but they are to compel no one since no one can be compelled to believe the opposite of what he or she thinks at heart is true. If some one believes differently from the clergy and makes no trouble, then he or she is to be left in peace. But if someone does make trouble, then he or she is to be separated since this is a matter of order that is the reason for having a clergy.

Arcana Coelestia 10794–10796; 10798

Useful means for accepting what is spiritual from the Lord include all the functions of religion and, therefore, of worship: the things, therefore, that teach an appreciation and recognition of what is good and true and that, therefore, teach eternal life. People derive similar things from parental discipline, teachers, sermons, and books, and especially by the consistent effort to live by them. In Christendom, this happens through teaching and preaching from the Word and, through the Word, from the Lord.

Divine Love and Wisdom 333

Baptism was established to be a sign that a person belonged to the church and as a reminder of the need for regeneration, baptism being really the spiritual washing that is regeneration.
. . .

People who have been baptized should realize that baptism itself does not provide either faith or salvation; it bears witness to the fact that they receive faith and are saved if they are regenerated.

The New Jerusalem and Its Heavenly Doctrine 202; 207

The Holy Supper was established by the Lord as a means to the union of the church with heaven and, therefore, with the Lord, so it is the holiest form of worship.

But people do not grasp how it is a means to this union unless they know something about the inner or spiritual meaning of the Word, for otherwise their thinking does not go beyond the outward meaning, which is the literal meaning. . . In that [inner] meaning, the body or flesh of the Lord is the goodness of love, as is the bread; and the Lord's blood is the goodness of faith, as is the wine; and the eating is internalizing [*appropriatio*] and union. . . .

But it needs to be realized that this happens only with people who are involved in the goodness of love and faith in the

119

Lord, from the Lord. For them, there is a union by means of the Holy Supper: for others, there is a presence but not a union.

The New Jerusalem and Its Heavenly Doctrine 210–213

We have already stated and demonstrated that inner worship (which stems from love and compassion) is actual worship and that outward worship without this internal is no worship at all. Rather, rendering inner worship external is making external worship more necessary than inner worship, which is an inversion of priorities. It is like saying that there is no inner worship apart from the outward when the fact is that there is no outward worship apart from the inner. . . . All outward worship is a formal version of the inner since the inner is the actual essential. Worshiping according to the form without its essence is rendering the inner external. For example, [it would be saying that] if someone lived where there was no church, no preaching, no sacraments, no clergy, then he or she could not be saved or have any worship when the fact is that such a person can inwardly worship the Lord. But it does not follow that the external ought to be lacking.

To make all this clearer, let us take as an example making the essence of worship consist of attending church, observing the sacraments, listening to sermons, praying, following the church calendar, and other outward and ceremonial practices, persuading oneself that this is adequate, talking about faith, all of which are formalities of worship. People who make worship from love and compassion the essential behave in the same way . . . with even greater diligence and care, but they do not make this the essential of worship. Because there is inward worship within their outward observances, there is something holy and alive. . . The actual essential is what brings holiness and life into the formal or ceremonial.

Arcana Coelestia 1175

CHAPTER 10

The Divine

.

Now we should be able to deal with the most controversial topic, that of the nature of God, without having to fight through the usual baggage of "God-language." There is no room whatever in Swedenborgian theology for God the tyrant, God the immense, remote figure with the long white beard, God the implacable judge, God the landlord who, in C. S. Lewis's scathing image, loves his tenants dearly and will damn them to eternal torment if they break one of his millions of impossible rules.

Swedenborg insisted that the human mind could not comprehend the Divine "as it is in itself." In this, he would concur with the mystics of the *via negativa* who center their process on denying the adequacy of any statement about God. He parts company with such mystics, though, in his belief that the Divine accommodates itself to our comprehension; and he spends far more time talking about what we can know than about what we cannot.

The most accurate thing we can say about the Divine, given the limitations of our understanding, is that it is infinite "love-and-wisdom." The love is the energy that constitutes the substance of all creation, and the wisdom is the order or design that is everywhere present and in some measure perceptible to the truly inquiring mind. In one sense, then, Swedenborg's God is the very pattern of the universe; but this must not be construed impersonally. The very pattern, for him, is essentially personal, i.e., loving, wise, and creative.

In our own immediate experience, then, the most adequate

models we have for understanding the Divine are the models provided by genuinely loving and perceptive individuals, or even by ourselves when we are at our best. In our less direct experience, though, we have the most adequate model in the figure of Jesus, who is seen as God entering our own nature and transforming it. There can be absolutely no thought here of a son sacrificing himself to allay the wrath of an angry father. This *is* the Father speaking through the Son, and as the Gospels insist on a number of occasions, the love and insight that Jesus manifested toward all are the love and insight of the Father.

The result is a Christ who is unique not so much in kind as in degree, who carries to infinite power the same qualities and process to which we ourselves are called. Here, if you will, we are at the very center of the theology, the point at which it all comes to focus.

General Considerations

All the elements of human reason converge and, so to speak, focus in this—that there is one God who is the creator of the universe. So the person who possesses reason neither does nor can think otherwise. Tell someone of sound reason that there are two creators of the universe and you will feel a resistance from that individual within yourself, simply from the sound of his or her voice in your ears. . . .

Can anyone whose reason is healthy fail to perceive that the Divine is not divided, that there is no plurality of infinite, uncreated, omnipotent beings or gods?

Divine Love and Wisdom 23; 27

If you gather everything known and submit it to the insight of your mind and, in some elevation of spirit, explore what everything has in common, you can only conclude that this is love and wisdom. These are, in fact, the two essentials of human life. Everything we have that is civic, everything moral, and everything spiritual depends on these two and is nothing without them. This holds true also of all the elements of the life of the aggregate person, which is . . . the larger or smaller community, the kingdom or empire, the church, and also the angelic heaven. Take love and wisdom away from them, and think whether they are anything, and you will grasp the fact that, without these as their source, they are nothing.

No one can deny that love and wisdom together are in God in their essence. From the love within himself, he loves everyone; and from the wisdom within himself, he leads everyone. Seen in its [overall] design, the created universe is so full of wisdom from love that you could say that, taken all together, all its contents are that wisdom itself. It contains countless things in such a design, both sequential and simultaneous, that, taken all together, they make one. There is no other way it could be held together and constantly maintained.

Divine Love and Wisdom   28–29

Out of·his divine love or mercy, the Lord wants to have everyone near him, so that they do not stand outside the doors (that is, in the lowest heaven)—he wants them to come into the highest heaven and, if possible, to be not only with him but within him. This is the nature of divine love, or the Lord's love.

Arcana Coelestia   1799:2

God alone—therefore, the Lord—is love itself because he is life itself, and angels and mortals are recipients of life. . . .

[F]or this to come within the reach of discernment, we must at all costs realize that the Lord, being love in its own essence (that is, divine love), is visible to angels in heaven as a sun and that warmth and light emanate from that sun and that the emanating warmth in its essence is love and the emanating light in its essence is wisdom. We must realize that angels are receptive of that spiritual warmth and spiritual light to the extent that they are instances of love and wisdom—not instances of love and wisdom in their own right [*se*],but from the Lord.

That spiritual warmth and spiritual light do not flow into and affect angels only but also flow into and affect mortals, precisely to the extent that we are receptive. We are receptive in proportion to our love of the Lord and our love toward the neighbor.

Divine Love and Wisdom   4–5

Once the world was created, God was in space but not bound by space and in time but not bound by time. God, and the divine [power] that emanates directly from God, is not in space but is omnipresent, with everyone in the world and with every angel in heaven and every spirit under heaven, which cannot be grasped in any merely natural concept but can to some extent be grasped in spiritual concepts. . . . The reason God is present in space but not bound by space and in time but not bound by time is that God is always the same, from eternity to eternity, with no change in essential quality after creation from before.

True Christian Religion 30

The fact that the Divine or God is not within space (even though it is omnipresent and is in every individual in the world, every angel in heaven, and every spirit below heaven) cannot be grasped with any merely natural concept, but it can be grasped with a spiritual concept. . . . A spiritual concept does not derive anything from space but gets its whole nature from state. State is predicated of love, of life, of wisdom, of affections and their derived pleasures—in general, of the good and the true.

A truly spiritual concept about these things has nothing in common with space. It is higher and looks at concepts of space as lower than itself the way heaven looks at earth.

Divine Love and Wisdom 7

People who do not know that God transcends time and who cannot think from some perception of this fact are wholly unable to grasp eternity except as an eternity of time; and then they cannot help thinking nonsense about a God from eternity. They are actually thinking on the basis of a beginning, and a beginning is strictly a matter of time. Their folly is that God came into being from himself, which readily lapses into thinking about nature as originating in itself. The only way out of this is through a spiritual or angelic concept of eternity, which transcends time; and once time is transcended, then the eternal and the Divine are the same, the Divine being divine in

124

itself and not from itself. . . . That which is "in itself" is the actual reality that is the source of everything. Intrinsic reality is life itself, which is the divine love of the divine wisdom and the divine wisdom of the divine love. To angels, this is the eternal—transcending time, therefore, the way the uncreated transcends the created or the infinite the finite, with no ratio possible between them.

Divine Love and Wisdom 76

We can see, then, how sense-bound is the thinking of people who believe that nature has come into being on its own—that is, how exclusively they trust their physical senses and the shadows these cast on spiritual matters. They are thinking from the eye and not from their understanding. Thinking from the eye closes the understanding, but thinking from the understanding opens the eye.

Divine Love and Wisdom 46

GOD IS ESSENTIAL PERSON

In all the heavens, there is no concept of God that is not a concept of a person. This is because heaven *in toto* and in detail is like a person in form, and the Divine that is within angels constitutes heaven. Further, their thought proceeds according to heaven's form; so it is impossible for angels to think about God in any other way. . . . This is why everyone in this world who is united to heaven thinks this way about God when he or she is "centered" [*in se*] or in his or her spirit. Because God is person, all angels and all spirits are people in perfect form. Heaven's form causes this, being like itself in its largest and in its smallest instances.

Divine Love and Wisdom 11

The Lord's life, as we have said, is divine love—that is, a love for the whole human race, [willing] that, if possible, the whole—that everyone—be saved forever. People who do not have the Lord's love, that is, who do not love the neighbor as themselves, never have the Lord's life, which means that they are not born from him. . . .

Arcana Coelestia 1803

[T]he Lord, who is the God of the universe, is uncreated and infinite, while mortals and angels are created and finite. And since the Lord is uncreated and infinite, he is that reality [*Esse*] itself called Jehovah and is life itself or intrinsic life. No one can be created directly from the uncreated, infinite, essential reality and intrinsic life because the Divine is one and not divided: our creation must occur by means of things created and limited, so formed that the Divine can be in them. Since mortals and angels are of this nature, they are recipients of life.

Divine Love and Wisdom 4

Presence and Power

God alone acts: we let ourselves be acted upon and react to all intents with apparent independence, although this too, more inwardly, comes from God.

The Intercourse between the Soul and the Body 14

The Lord is, in fact, present with everyone, for there is no other source of life; and he oversees the smallest details for everyone, even for the worst people and for people in hell. The mode [of his presence] varies, though, depending on their acceptance [of him]. With people who accept the life of his love . . . obliquely and corrupt it into loves of the evil and false, he is present and is guiding their purposes toward the good to the extent that he can, but his presence with them is called absence, to the extent that [their] evil is remote from the good and their falsity, from the true.

Arcana Coelestia 2706

God is omnipresent from the first to the most remote elements of his design. The means of God's omnipresence from the first to the most remote elements of his design is the warmth and light from the spiritual world's sun, which surrounds him. The design was realized by means of this sun; and from it, he sends forth a warmth and light that pervade the universe from its first to its most remote elements, producing the life that belongs to humans, to all animals, and even that vegetative soul that is in every seed on earth. These two [spiritual warmth and light] flow into every one, making each subject live and grow according to the design given it from its creation. And since God is not spatially extended and yet fills all the expanses of the universe, he is omnipresent.

We have shown elsewhere that God is in all space without [being bound by] space and in all time without [being bound by] time. Since this is the case, he perceives everything by his omnipresence, provides everything by his omniscience, and manages everything by his omnipotence. So we can see that omnipresence, omniscience, and omnipotence make a one or that each presupposes the others, so that they can in no way be separated from each other.

True Christian Religion 63

We are led and taught by the Lord alone through and from the angelic heaven. We do say that we are led through and from the angelic heaven, but the leading "through" is [description] from appearance, while leading "from" is [description] from the truth. The reason it seems as though we are led through the angelic heaven is that the Lord seems to be above that heaven as a sun. The reason the truth is that we are led from heaven is that the Lord is within that heaven as the soul is within a person. The Lord is actually omnipresent and not in space, as we have shown earlier, so distance is an appearance that depends on union with him. The union depends on our acceptance of love and wisdom from him.

And since no one can be united to the Lord as he is in himself, he, therefore, looks to angels at a distance like a sun. Still, he is within the whole angelic heaven like a soul in a person. In the same way, he is within each community of heaven and within each individual angel there. The human soul is, in fact, not only the soul of the whole but the soul of each single part.

Divine Providence 162

The reason we are in God through a life in accord with [his] design is that God is present everywhere in the universe, in its each and every detail: he is in its inmost things, since these are in accord with [his] design. In things that are not in accord with the design, however (which are those things only that are outside the inmost things), God is everywhere present through a ceaseless struggle against them and through a ceaseless effort to bring them back into the design.

For this reason, insofar as we let ourselves be brought back into the design, God is omnipresent in us and we are in God. God's absence from us is no more possible than is the absence of the sun from the earth through its warmth and light. But its objects enjoy their proper efficacy [*virtute*] only as they accept these two emanations from that sun, which happens in spring and summer time.

True Christian Religion 70:2

[I]t is an abiding truth that everything good—and, therefore, everything true—comes from the Lord. Angels are involved in this perception, even to the extent that they perceive how fully the goodness and truth of anything comes from the Lord and its evil and falsity from themselves. They actually confess this to newly arrived souls and to spirits who are doubtful about it. They go even further, confessing that they are withheld by the Lord from the evil and false things that stem from their own self-image and are kept involved in what is good and true. This restraint and this inflow are perceptible to them. . . . The reason we think that we do what is good and think what is true on our own is that it seems that way because we are in an utterly unperceptive state and in a profound darkness as to the inflow. So, we draw our conclusions from the appearance, from an illusion from which we can never let ourselves be withdrawn as long as we trust only our senses and debate about the truth. Still, we ought to do what is good and think what is true as though we were doing it on our own, for there is no other way we can be reformed and regenerated.

Arcana Coelestia 2016

We cannot grasp how the Lord is in an angel and an angel in the Lord unless we know what union is like. The union is

128

one of the Lord with the angel and one of the angel with the Lord.

The angels' part in this process is as follows. Nothing in angels' perception contradicts the appearance that they are involved in love and wisdom on their own, just as we are, and, therefore, that love and wisdom are theirs as possessions. If their perception were not like this, no union would occur, so the Lord would not be in them nor they in the Lord.

It cannot happen that the Lord is in any angel or person unless that individual in whom the Lord is present in love and wisdom perceives these as his or her own. In this way, the Lord is not only accepted but, having been accepted, is kept and is also loved in return. This, then, is how an angel becomes wise and stays wise.

Who can love the Lord and the neighbor and who can want to be wise, unless he feels and perceives what he loves, learns, and gains as his? Who can keep anything in himself otherwise? If it were not like this, then the inflowing love and wisdom would have no seat; they would just flow through without making any difference. So, an angel would not be an angel nor a person, a person. They would simply be like something that is inanimate.

Divine Love and Wisdom   115

In *Divine Love and Wisdom*, we showed that the Lord is divine love and divine wisdom. . . . Since what emanates from the Divine is the Divine itself, and divine providence is the primary emanation, it follows that to act contrary to the laws of divine providence would be to act contrary to the Divine itself. We can also say that the Lord is providence, . . . since divine providence is the divine design as it focuses particularly on our salvation.

Divine Providence   331

If we were born into the love into which we were [first] created, we would not be involved in any evil or even know what evil is. . . . But since love toward the neighbor has been changed into love of self, and this love has grown in strength, human love has been changed into bestial love, and people have become animals rather than humans—except that we can think about what the body is sensing, tell one thing from another, and can be taught. We can become civic and moral people and, ultimately, spiritual people. . . .

Divine Providence   275–276

[Our] evils cannot be removed unless they come to light. This does not mean that we are to do them so that they will come to light but that we should take stock of ourselves—not just our actions but our thoughts and what we would do if we were not afraid of the laws and of dishonor. . . .

Divine Providence   278

So evils are tolerated [under providence] *for a purpose—our salvation.. . .*

Divine Providence   281

The Lord could heal everyone's discernment and work things so that we thought good things rather than evil ones, using various fears, miracles, conversations with the dead, visions, and dreams. . . . But if only our discernment were healed, we would be like corpses that have been embalmed or covered with aromatic herbs and roses. . . .

Divine Providence   282

[D]ivine providence is in the most minute details of our thoughts and affections, which means that we cannot think or intend anything on our own.

Divine Providence   287

The goal of divine providence is a heaven from the human race. . . . Divine love—and, therefore, divine providence—has the goal of a heaven made up of people who have become angels and who are becoming angels, people to whom it can give all the blessings and joys attendant on love and wisdom, giving them from itself in the individuals. It can do nothing else

130

because its image and likeness are in them from creation, its image in them being wisdom and its likeness in them being love. The Lord within them is love united to wisdom and wisdom united to love.

Divine Providence 27

Accommodation

We mentioned earlier that, even though the doctrine of faith is intrinsically divine and, therefore, beyond human or even angelic grasp, still, in the Word, things have been composed in a rational mode according to human comprehension. It is like a parent who is teaching little boys and girls and who, in teaching, explains everything on their level [*secundum genium eorum*]. Otherwise, it would be like teaching something that was not learned or like casting seed upon rocks. Or it is like the angels who teach simple-hearted folk in the other life. Even though these angels are involved in heavenly and spiritual wisdom, they still do not elevate themselves above the grasp of the people they are teaching, but talk with them in simple terms, still pressing gradually upwards as they teach. If they were to talk from their angelic wisdom, the simple folk would not understand anything at all and would, therefore, not be led toward the true and good aspects of faith. It would be the same if the Lord had not taught the Word in a rational mode according to human comprehension.

Arcana Coelestia 2533:2

[When the Bible says] that "we should not climb up any other way" [John 10:1ff], [it] means we cannot climb up to God the Father because he is invisible; and, therefore, we can neither reach him nor be united to him. This is why he came into the world and made himself visible, accessible, and open to union with us—it was for the sole purpose of our salvation. For unless God is approached as a person in our thought, every concept of God is destroyed and vanishes like sight

looking off into the universe. It vanishes into an empty noth-
ingness or into nature or into whatever we encounter in
nature.

True Christian Religion 538

"[T]he glory in the cloud" is the Divine-True that has not
been . . . accommodated to [our] grasp, being above sensory
illusions and appearances. . . . The Divine-True is not of one
level only but of many.* The Divine-True on its first level and
also on its second level is that which emanates directly from
the Lord. This is above angelic understanding. The Divine-
True on the third level, though, is the kind that occurs in the
inmost or third heaven. It is of a kind that cannot be grasped
at all by mortals. The Divine-True in the fourth level is the
kind that occurs in the intermediate or second heaven, and
this is not intelligible to mortals either. But the Divine-True
on the fifth level is the kind that exists in the farthest or first
heaven. This can, to some extent, be grasped by mortals if
they are enlightened, but it is still of such a nature that much
of it is beyond the power of human words to express; and
when it does fit into concepts, it creates an ability to perceive
and to believe that things are as they actually are. But the Divine-True on the sixth level is the kind that exists among mortals and is adapted to their perception, like the literal meaning
of the Word. This meaning or this truth is pictured by the
cloud and the more inward truths, by the glory within the
cloud.

Arcana Coelestia 8443

The blessedness that is eternity in its highest sense cannot
be defined except by its correspondence with things in the
human realm, for things that are divine or infinite cannot be
grasped except by using finite ones of which we can have some
concept. Without some concept drawn from finite things
(specifically, without some concept drawn from matters of
space and time), we can understand nothing about divine

---

*These are presented as levels of reality above those described in chapter 3,
"Alternate Realities."

things, let alone about the infinite. We cannot even think at all without some concept from space and time . . . because physically—and, therefore, in thoughts based on sensory externals—we are in time.

Arcana Coelestia   3938

[E]veryone knows that the Divine is never in darkness but is in light since the Divine is light itself. So when it is said that [the Divine is in] darkness, this is relative to people who are not in any light. For to them, the divine truths that constitute heaven's light have no other appearance. They do not believe them; they actually deny them. The Divine is visible to everyone according to the quality of his or her life and faith—as light to people who are in light, then, and as darkness to people who are in darkness.

Arcana Coelestia   8928:4

There are three things that follow in order—*accommodation, application, and union.* Accommodation must happen before there can be application and application together with accommodation before there can be union; and the accommodation on God's part was that he became human.

True Christian Religion   370:3

Later on, I saw some spirits from the same planet in a lower place and talked with them. . . . They were idolaters, worshiping a stone image—in human form but unlovely. It needs to be realized that all the people who arrive in the other life have at first the same kind of worship they had in the world but that they are gradually removed from it. The reason is that all worship stays rooted in the deeper levels of human life and can be removed and erased from them only gradually.

When I saw what was happening, I was allowed to tell them that it was not permissible to revere anything dead, only something living. They answered that they knew that God was alive and that the stone was not but that they thought about the living God when they looked at the humanoid stone and that this was the only way they could direct their thought-concepts toward an invisible God. Then I was allowed to tell them that thought-concepts can be directed and focused toward an invisible God when they are directed and focused toward the Lord, who is the visible God, and that in this way people can be united in thought and affection to the invisible God. . . .

Arcana Coelestia 9972

We need also to explain why the Lord himself, who is the Divine-Good itself and heaven's sun itself, is called the mediator and intercessor with the Father. When the Lord was in the world, before he was fully glorified, he was the Divine-True, so there was a mediation and he did intercede with the Father—that is, with the actual Divine-Good. . . . But after he was glorified as to his human [nature], then he was called the mediator and intercessor because people cannot think about the intrinsic Divine except by setting up some concept of a divine person. It is even less possible to be united to the intrinsic Divine by love without some such concept. If we think about the intrinsic Divine without some concept of a divine person, we think without boundaries, and a concept without boundaries is no concept at all. . . .

The intrinsic Divine cannot be grasped in any concept. . . . But, notably, people who think about God from themselves or from the flesh all think about him without boundaries—that is, without any defined concept, while people who do not think about God from themselves or from the flesh but from the spirit think about him with boundaries. That is, they set up for themselves a concept of the Divine in human guise. This is how angels in heaven think about God, and it is also how wise people thought in early times. When the Divine appeared to them, it did so as a divine person since the Divine is a divine person as it passes through heaven. The reason is that heaven is the universal human. . . . We can see from this the quality of intellectuals in this world and the quality of intellectuals in heaven. Intellectuals in this world distance themselves from any personal concept [of God], so there is no mediation between their minds and the Divine, which brings darkness on them. But intellectuals in heaven have a concept of the Divine

in a human; so the Lord serves as their mediator and is, therefore. a light for their minds.

Arcana Coelestia 8705:4–5

The Process of Incarnation

From the first creation, [God] was in a human [nature] and in
a human [nature] from himself—namely, in the entirety of
heaven, which taken all together reflects a single person. But
this was not his own proper [human nature] because it was in
heaven's angels. In the Divine-Human, though, he is in his
own proper [human nature].

The Athanasian Creed 119

The intrinsic Divine in heaven, or in the universal human,
was the Divine-Human, and this is how Jehovah himself was
clothed with a human [form]. But when the human race
reached the point that it could no longer be influenced by the
intrinsic Divine clothed as a Divine-Human (that is, when
Jehovah could no longer reach people because they had
moved so far away), then Jehovah (who is the Lord as to divine essence) came down and by divine conception and a
unique virgin birth took a humanity upon himself.

Arcana Coelestia 3061:2

I have been told that, in the Lord from eternity, who is
Jehovah, before he took on a humanity in this world, the two
higher levels were actual and the third level was potential, as
they are with angels; but that after he took on a human
[nature] in this world, he added on the third level, which is
called natural. In this way, he became a person like other people in the world, but with the difference that this [third] level,
like the others, was infinite and uncreated, while these levels in
angels and mortals are finite and created.

Divine Love and Wisdom 233

[A]lmost all the people who come [into the other life] from
Christendom have a concept of three gods, even though they

have said out loud that there is only one God. For it is not human to think "one" when the concept of "three" has gained entrance in advance and when each of these is called God and is distinguished from the others as to attributes and gifts—and is even worshiped separately. This is why there is a worship of three gods at heart, while there is one in mouth only. It is recognized in Christendom that the whole trinity is in the Lord, but still [Christians] in the other life do not think about the Lord very much. Actually, his humanity is a real problem to many of them because they separate it from his Divine and do not believe that it is divine.

Arcana Coelestia   3704:7

[T]he inner and the outer of a human being are two distinct things, but they are united to each other. The inner acts within and into the outer, but it does not act through the outer. The inner actually takes thousands of things into consideration, of which the outer selects only those things that suit its purposes. In a person's internal (by which we mean the intentional and perceptive mind), there are collections of concepts so vast that if they were to flow out through a person's mouth, it would be like a blast from a bellows. . . .

It is the same with the Divine and the human of the Lord. The Father's Divine is actually the soul of his human, and the human is its body. The human does not ask its Divine to tell it what to say and do.

True Christian Religion   154:5

The uniting of the Lord's human essence with his divine essence did not happen all at once but went on through the whole course of his life, from infancy to the end of his life in this world. So, he climbed constantly toward glorification— that is, toward being one. . . .

Arcana Coelestia   2033

God could not use his omnipotence to rescue us except by becoming human; and he could not make his human divine except by having his human be first born like the human of an infant, then like that of a child, and later by having that human form itself into a vessel and dwelling into which the Father could enter. This was accomplished by his fulfillment of all things of the Word—that is, all the laws of the [divine] design that it contains. To the extent that he did accomplish this, he made himself one with the Father, and the Father made himself one with him.

True Christian Religion 73:3

[W]e have already stated several times that the intrinsic Divine or Jehovah was in [the Lord] because he was conceived by Jehovah, which is why he called him his father and himself, his son. But [to the extent that] the Lord was involved in the frail humanity he had inherited from his mother, . . . Jehovah or the intrinsic Divine that was within him seemed to be absent, while to the extent that the Lord was involved in his glorified human or his human made divine, Jehovah or the intrinsic Divine was present and was in his actual human.

Arcana Coelestia 7058:3

We have stated and explained earlier that the Lord had two states while he was in the world, a state of humiliation and a state of glorification. His state of humiliation came when he was involved in the humanity he had gotten from his mother and his state of glorification, when he was involved in the Divine that he received from Jehovah his father. The former state . . . he left behind completely; and he put on a divine human when he left this world and returned to the essential Divine he had been in from eternity. . . .

Arcana Coelestia 2288

The reason the Lord had these two states, one of emptiness and one of glorification, was that this was the only way he could progress toward becoming one, since this is in accord with the divine design, which is unchangeable. The divine design is that we should arrange ourselves to accept God and prepare ourselves as vessels and dwellings into which God may enter and where he may live as in his temple.

137

We are to do this in apparent independence, still acknowledging that it all comes from God. We are to acknowledge this
because we do not feel God's presence and working, even
though God is most intimately accomplishing everything that
is good in love and everything that is true in faith. Everyone
moves and must move according to this design in order to become spiritual instead of natural.

The Lord moved in the same way in order to make his natural human divine. This is why he prayed to the Father, why
he did his will, why he credited everything he did and said to
the Father, and why he said on the cross, "My God, my God,
why have you deserted me?" In this state, God does indeed
seem to be absent.

But after this state, there comes another, a state of union
with God. In this latter state, we act as before, but we are then
acting from God. There is no longer any need to credit God
with everything good that we intend and do and everything
true that we think and say, because this is written on our
hearts and is, therefore, inherent in our every action and
word.

This is how the Lord united himself to his Father and the
Father united him with himself. In a word, the Lord glorified
his human (that is, made it divine) the way the Lord regener-
ates us (that is, makes us spiritual).

True Christian Religion 105

[T]he Lord's whole life in the world, from earliest childhood, was a constant temptation-trial and a constant victory,
the last being when he prayed for his enemies on the cross,
praying, therefore, for all people in all corners of the globe.
. . . Every temptation-trial is an assault on the love a person is
involved in: the level of the love determines the level of the
trial. If a love is not attacked, then there is no trial. . . . The
Lord's life was a love for the whole human race and was so
great and so perfect that it was nothing but pure love. This life
of his was subject to constant trials, as we have said, from earliest childhood to his last hour in the world. . . . [H]e was at-

tacked by all the hells, which he consistently resisted, con-
trolled, and conquered, simply and solely from his love toward
the whole human race. Since this love is not human but divine
and since the amount of the love determines the amount of
the temptation-trial, we can draw our conclusions about the
severity of his struggles and the ferocity of the hells. I know
the truth of this for certain.

Arcana Coelestia 1690

It is an *arcanum* hitherto undisclosed that ultimately the
Lord fought against angels themselves, in fact with the whole
angelic heaven. But the situation is like this. Angels are involved in the highest wisdom and intelligence, but all their
wisdom and intelligence comes from the Lord's Divine. On
their own, or from their own self-consciousness, they have no
wisdom or intelligence. . . . They themselves openly admit
this. . . . Angels also say that their whole selfhood is evil and
false, both from heredity and from their actual lives in the
world while they were mortals. . . . Since this is the case, in
order for the Lord to bring the entirety of heaven back into
the heavenly design, he had also to be subjected to trials in
himself from the angels, who, to the extent that they are involved in their self-image, are not involved in the good and
the true. These temptation-trials are the deepest of all, since
they act solely into purposes, with such subtlety that they cannot be detected.

Arcana Coelestia 4295:2

In order to make the human divine by following the usual
course, the Lord was willing to be born like anyone else, to be
taught and reborn like anyone else, but with a difference. The
difference is that we are reborn by the Lord, while the Lord
not only reconceived [literally, "regenerated"] himself but actually glorified himself, that is, made himself divine. As we are
made new by the inflow of compassion and faith, the Lord was
made new by the inflow of the divine love that was within him
and was his own. This means we can see that our regeneration

is an image of the Lord's glorification or (which amounts to the same thing) that we can see in the process of our own regeneration a kind of image, however distant, of the Lord's glorification.

Arcana Coelestia 3138

There is only one life, and it comes from the Lord alone. Angels, spirits, and mortals are only recipients of life. This has been made known to me from so much experience that there is not the slightest doubt left. . . . Our appropriation of the Lord's life comes from his love and mercy toward the whole human race, from the fact that he wants to give himself and what is his to each individual, and that he actually does so to the extent that we accept it—that is, to the extent that we are involved in lives of goodness and lives of truth, as images and likenesses of him.

Arcana Coelestia 3742

EPILOGUE

·

In his doctoral thesis on Friedreich Schelling and Emanuel Swedenborg, Friedemann Horn quotes the German scholar K.C.F. Krause: "If only all the divisions of christendom could agree on the simple, devout, ethical teaching that Swedenborg expressed so lucidly and cogently, that true Christianity is the observance of God's laws in the spirit of love!"* Swedenborg, I believe, would agree wholeheartedly and would urge us to see the intricacies and subtleties of his theological system as a defense of that simplicity against the intricate and subtle rationalizations that may arise from a sophisticated materialism.

But that is not all. Swedenborg did not prize simplicity for its own sake. In good biblical fashion, his view of the goal, whether for an individual or for the human race, was not a return to Eden but the descent of the Holy City. He delighted in all new discoveries: for example, in the increasingly detailed understanding of the physical world that his microscope offered. Theologically, as he found the fullest development of intellect to be inseparable from the fullest devotion to love, he also found the fullest expression of love to be inseparable from the fullest development of intellect.

In his *Essay on Man*, Alexander Pope wrote the familiar lines

> Know then thyself, presume not God to scan;
> The proper study of mankind is man.
> Epistle II, 1–2

*Translated from Friedemann Horn, *Schelling und Swedenborg: Ein Beitrag zur Problemgeschichte des deutschen Idealismus und zur Geschichte Swedenborgs in Deutschland* (Zurich, Switzerland: Swedenborg Verlag, 1954), 3.

For Swedenborg, the objects of the "studies" that Pope sees as mutually exclusive come together in the figure of the glorified Christ. We may not presume to scan the Divine, but the Divine has bridged the gap and, in a sense, made itself available to be scanned. it is not just that the Gospels command us to love; it is that the person of Jesus embodies divine love. If we "study" that embodiment—using "study in that full sense it bears in the line, "I ain't gonna study war no more"—we learn how to live with each other and with ourselves.

This is Christianity with a difference. Seen through the lens of this theology, the Jesus of the Gospels is very much in process. Love is not a "state" so much as it is an energy, an energy with an intrinsic direction. Further, to put it bluntly, in the case of Jesus, the process leads to absolute perfection, to a oneness with the Divine so complete that even the physical body is transformed. Any attempt to see Jesus as simply an improved version of ourselves shatters against his resurrection.

Lastly, at least for present purposes, the Jesus of Swedenborgian theology is intellectually brilliant. He has not only the most compassionate heart but also the most precise, retentive, and penetrating *mind*. In *Arcana Coelestia* 4329:2, Swedenborg distinguishes between "obscure" general ideas, characteristic of minds that have little information, and clear general ideas, characteristic of minds that are learned. This wise simplicity or "innocence of wisdom" is his ideal. There is the skillful popularizer who can make us feel as though we understand. There is a mid-range intelligence that can expound ideas that can be understood only by other mid-range intelligences. Then, there is the profound brilliance that can shine through to total clarity.

Jesus' field of study was the human soul, not in some kind of oversimplified laboratory isolation but in all its living relationships to its companions and to its source. The supply of raw data for such a study is overwhelming. No one before Jesus or since has comprehended that data so perfectly or spoken so clearly and precisely to its essence. Try rewriting the Sermon on the Mount.

INDEX OF WORKS CITED

143

INDEX

.